The First-Ever Interview
Between Man & Money

Bill Quain, Ph.D.

Money Talks...Finally!

By Bill Quain, Ph.D.

© Copyright 2015 Bill Quain, Ph.D.

ISBN: 978-0-9623646-8-6

Cover Design and Layout by Parry Design Studio, Inc.

www.parrydesign.com

Acknowledgements

First of all, let me acknowledge the incredible contributions from Money. He was absolutely fabulous, and gave me so much of his time. Money, I thank you. It wasn't easy to find you, but when I did, it was well worth it.

I would also like to mention that some members of Money's family were crucial to the success of this book. There is nothing like family, and Money's family added some excellent comments and insights. In particular, I would like to thank his *Uncle Buck* and *Aunt Penny*. They never lacked for *interest* in the project. They gave up a lot of their time, even though they are busy ranchers—raising prize *cash cows*.

Uncle Buck and *Aunt Penny* have a couple of children who also contributed, although I had to sort through the *notes* they gave me. Money's cousin *Fast Money*, along with his sister *Easy Money*, made a lot of *cents* to me. After listening to them, I was ready to *change*.

In addition to Money and his family, Jack and Elizabeth Parry did their usual, exceptional job with the layout, design and artwork. My sister Jeannine Norris (a best-selling children's author) was my go-to editor of choice, *again*. Thanks Jeannine!

My agent Katherine Glover kept me on the straight and narrow again with this book. Katherine, let's spread the Money concept worldwide. People need this message, and you are just the person to launch this to the people who need it most. As always, Katherine has the contacts and relationships that she spent years building. Thanks Katherine.

Steve Trauger, owner of STVP (Seriously Total Video Productions), was there every step of the way to produce my promotional videos. Steve is pretty famous in this area for his coverage of events like the Miss America Pageant. Thanks Steve. It is a blast to work with you. If anyone needs videos or other work, Steve is your man!

Many friends and family members (too many to mention here, for fear of missing one or two) gave me fantastic support as I wrote this book. Thanks everyone.

Finally, my wife Jeanne jumped in to do the final editing and rewrite. It was just like old times Jeanne. As always, I am impressed with your ability to sit through the many hours of listening to my theories, rantings and ravings.

Dedication

I am pleased and honored to dedicate this book to my wife Jeanne, and to my two daughters Amanda and Kathleen. I am one lucky guy.

Contents

Introduction ix
   A Message From Money

Chapter 1 1
   One Boss or Many Customers?

Chapter 2 5
   Want More Money? Build Equity

Chapter 3 17
   Your Job is Fixed Income!

Chapter 4 31
   Money Says: Command Me

Chapter 5 37
   Risk and Reward

Chapter 6 47
   Seven Secret Steps

Chapter 7 53
   Add Value to the Solution

Chapter 8 59
   Survivor, Money Edition

Chapter 9 63
   Money Talks About Customers

Chapter 10 69
   Money Talks About Price

Chapter 11 73
   Money Talks About Using Good Examples to Add Value

Summary 77
   Bill Quain Sums it Up

Outtakes from My Conversation with Money 87
   (Money Puts in his Own Two Cents)

Introduction

A Message From Money

I am so excited to finally have the opportunity to speak directly to ordinary men and women. Let me start off by saying a big "Thank you!" to Bill Quain. I think you should give him a big "Thank You" as well. After all, it was Bill who found me and gave me the opportunity to have this conversation with you.

Who am I? My name is Money and I want to be your friend. In fact, I want to come and spend time with each and every one of you reading this book. You see, most humans don't give me much thought. Oh, they'll get all excited and worried when they don't have enough of me, but most of the time, they just ignore me. And that's too bad, because I can really help you.

Why is there so much stress about money? That's an easy one to answer. You see, you need money. I pay the bills. I am the one that gets that credit card company to stamp "paid in full" on your monthly statement. You exchange me for food, shelter and clothing. You need me for vacations, and I am very handy to have around if you have an accident or get sick.

Most of you get up every morning and go to work for just one reason—to get a piece of me. You put up with crazy bosses, long hours, missed time with your children, and boring meetings, so that you can get a nice fat pile of me at the end of the week.

Hey, that's fine by me. I really like you and want to be your friend. I'd love to spend more time with you. I want to give you more confidence. In fact, being with you is a lot of fun because it makes me feel so good to be such a useful tool for you.

We all know that I am a great tool! But, that's all I am. I'm not the things you want. I am the tool you use to buy the things you want.

Now, this is very important: I am just not an ordinary tool. I am a power tool. That's right, a power tool. If you want to get things done, I am the power tool that gives you the power to accomplish your goals. You see, money gives you influence. Money gives you the power to change other people's lives.

So why are we strangers?

I can do all sorts of things for you and your family. But there is a big problem. You probably don't know that much about me. Oh sure, you know how useful I am for buying things. But, do you know how to get more of me? Do you understand what you need to do, so that you have an endless stream of money to do your bidding?

Let me tell you, I am really interested in getting to know you better. I want to spend time with you. I want to be your friend. I'd like to be out with you and your family. Take me on a cruise, to a nice restaurant, how about to college with your daughter, or to church to help others?

Having me around is a lot of fun. Got stress? Get Money!

Okay, so how do you get more of me?

I only have one mission in life—to help you. That's it. My life is pretty simple. I am ready, willing, and able to be the best tool you ever had. But in order for me to help you, you need more of me than you have now.

There are probably two things making it difficult for you to get more money. First, you don't know where I am now. Second, you don't know how to get me from where I am now to where you want me to be (with you!). Let's take a look at both of these points.

1. Where am I now? - Someone else has me. There are a few people who have a whole lot of me (rich people). I'm also with millions of ordinary people, but I am definitely out there in other people's pockets right now. That's where I am.

2. How do you get those people to give me to you? Well, that's the big question, isn't it? And that's where ordinary people really seem to get lost. Here's the good news: it isn't difficult. In fact, it is very simple.

That's what this book is all about

I was so excited when Bill Quain came along and gave me the opportunity to speak directly to you. I want to show you how to get other people to give you their money. Now don't get me wrong. There is nothing dishonest about that. In fact, if you want other people to consistently give you their money, you have to be brutally honest – with them and with yourself.

In this book, I am going to show you a simple system that will consistently trigger people to happily give you their money again and again.

In fact, if you follow this simple system, other people will demand that you let them give you their money.

You are going to have so much fun! Your life is going to be so much better. But guess what, if you do it right, the people who give you their money will be having fun as well. Their lives will be better. That's why they are going to give you their money.

They are Already Giving Their Money to Someone Else

Let me let you in on a big secret: right now, all of these people are giving their money to someone else. That's right. How do I know that? How can I be so sure? Well remember this: I am Money. Others are spending me, giving me to other people, and using me to buy things on the Internet. Money is flying all over the place. But unless you know how to trigger people to give you their money, you won't get much of it at all.

The problem is, they are not buying from you. But hey, don't get all flustered. All you need to do is find a way to make it easier for people to spend their money. And they will pay you for making their lives easier.

This is Going to be Fun

Bill Quain and I had a great time talking to each other. We both got very excited. Bill asked me all the questions that he thought you might want to ask. We spent a long time together talking about just one thing—how can ordinary men and women learn to make real money? After our talk, Bill wrote this book. He's good at that. He's written more than two-dozen best-selling books. His books have been translated and printed and sold all over the world.

You see, Bill understands how to make money. He knows that people will give them their money if he gives them exactly what they want and need. What is Bill's particular talent? He knows how to take complicated ideas and put them into simple, practical and useful words. Bill has a huge, loyal following of readers. They aren't bankers, Wall Street moguls, and politicians. No, Bill's readers are the real kind of people that need more money the most.

When Bill found me, he said he'd give me a voice. Imagine, Money finally has a voice! And Bill promised that he would put my voice into words, and it would make a difference in your life. It is practical advice for anyone who wants to change their lives by having more money.

Bill Quain and Money – one team

Folks, aren't you lucky? We started a winning team. We already have two members – an author who isn't afraid to tell you the truth, and Money – the most powerful tool you can ever have. We are looking for team members. We will take anyone on our team who is willing to listen, learn, and change. This team has only one goal: to win the money game. We are going to win the money game by helping people be happier. How will they become happier? They are going to send their money to you!

Sound crazy? Well, if you're still reading this book, you might just be crazy enough to learn how to get people to give you their money. And, when we say it like that, it doesn't sound crazy at all.

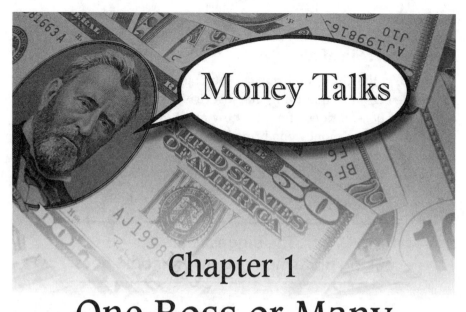

Chapter 1

One Boss or Many Customers?

Bill: Money, what is the biggest difference between a boss and a customer?

Money: That's easy Bill. A customer doesn't care how much money you make.

Bill: That's it folks. That's the big difference. You see, there is no question: your boss is a customer. Your boss has a problem and you solve it. When you solve the boss's problem, she/he commands money to jump out of her/his pocket and into yours. But, your boss is going to count every penny of that money. And the big boss is going to be watching your boss like a hawk.

If your boss is paying you too much money, the big boss (and the big, big boss, etc.) will be very unhappy. And if anybody else in your company finds out that you are making more than they make, *they* will be very unhappy. How will they express their unhappiness? Well, every situation is different, but I would be very careful the next time I opened my desk drawer.

The Biggest Sin of All

What is the thing that makes your boss most unhappy? I mean this is the big one—that thing that just drives bosses crazy. It happens with every boss. It doesn't matter how great the job you do. It doesn't matter how much money you bring into the company. It doesn't matter how happy you make the customers. Everyone in the whole world could love you, but if you commit this one great sin, your boss will be miserable.

The biggest sin:
Making more money than your boss does!

Did you ever wonder what is the maximum amount of money you can make on your job? Well, here is a hint. The maximum you can make is "a lot less than your boss makes." Find out what your boss makes, subtract a bunch of money from that amount, and that will tell you what your maximum is going to be. Well, of course your boss can't make any more than the big boss does. That's just the rule.

Can you see the difference between your boss's attitude and your customers' attitudes? Your boss is paying you for your time. Your customers—your real customers—are paying you to solve their problems.

Customers are Different

Your customers don't care how much money you make. All they care about is the value you bring to them. That's it. They will gladly pay you for every bit of **perceived value** that you bring to them. If they have a problem, and they have money, they are happy to pay you "whatever it takes" to get their problems solved. The more value you bring them, and the bigger the problem you solve, the more satisfied they are when they command money to jump out of their pockets and into yours.

And get this: your customers don't care if you are solving problems for other customers. As long as you continue to give them the attention they need, they don't care how many other people are paying you.

Your boss cares. Your boss will say, "I am paying you for your time. If I am paying you for your time, I want your undivided attention."

This means you can make more money with customers than you ever can with your boss. Why? It's because your boss and your customers think differently about the money you make.

That's why it is unlikely that you will solve your money problems by trading your time to a boss for dollars. If you want to make money—*and we mean real money*—keep your boss happy by doing a great job for her/him, but build equity by solving problems for customers. It's a win-win!

Money Talks

Chapter 2

Want More Money? Build Equity

Bill: Money, what's the best way for anyone to make more money?

Money: To build equity. Building equity is really the only way to make a lot more money, especially if you want to keep it coming in year after year.

What is Equity?

Money: Equity is something that you own and that makes you money. Smart people—people who want to make more money—will buy or build equity and then let that equity earn money for them.

Bill: When you say "equity," are you talking about the stock market or the bond market?

Money: Well, those are the kind of equities that most people think about. However, stock market and bond market equities are risky. In addition, most people don't handle their own investment equities. They give them to someone else to handle—like a stockbroker. There's nothing wrong with this, but if you really want to make a lot of money, you have to create different kinds of equity.

Bill: Money, I think you're right. Most humans don't have any idea that there are other kinds of equity to create out there. Since the purpose of equity is to create money (wealth) how about giving us your expert opinion on some other types of equities that people can develop?

---

1. Self equity
2. Customer equity
3. System equity
4. Network equity
5. Mentor equity

Money: Besides investment equities (stocks, bonds, and mutual funds) there are five other equities that people should invest in.

Bill: Wow, these look interesting! Before you tell us about the power of each one of these equities, would you explain why it is so important to build equity?

Money: That's a great question. I'm glad you asked. Let's talk a little bit about how equities work.

The only way to have a lot of money is to somehow break out of the "work an hour and get paid for an hour" mentality that holds so many people in a constant state of stress and worry. If you are trading your time for dollars, you can never get ahead, because you're always working for the next bit of money that you need.

The problem is: you only have so many hours in the day. And you stop making money when you sleep, go on vacation, or get sick. Are you getting the picture?

But, equity is different. When you buy or create equity, and put it to work for you, the equity works round-the-clock. In fact, equity never stops making money. Take a look at the humans in the following pictures. The first one (the worker) is making money. His shoveling makes the wheel turn, and money is generated. But when he stops shoveling, he stops making money because the wheel stops turning.

But look at the picture of the other man. He isn't a worker; he is a builder. He is building equity and then letting the equity work for him. He makes an investment in time and money and then lets his investment work for him. The investment never stops turning the wheel. Money is generated no matter what the man is doing. In this case he is sleeping in a hammock. But, he could be on the golf course, or at his daughter's recital, or doing anything he wants. He gained freedom because he built enough equity to work for him.

Bill: Money, are you saying that if people make the right investments they can have a choice about how they spend their time?

Money: That's right, they have choices. Now, most human beings don't have any choices because they are stuck on a job. They are told when to report to work, go home, and even retire.

However, if a person builds enough equity, and if it is the right kind of equity, the equity works for him or her. It takes time and money to build equity. It is important to remember that's what an investment is. You invest in something that is going to grow. If it is the right kind of investment, then what grows is money!

Bill: If investing in the right kind of equity is so powerful and produces such great results, why aren't people doing it all the time?

Money: I will give you the same answer time and time again during this interview.

The reason that people don't do the right things to help them make money? 1) They were never taught how to do it; 2) They never thought enough about it to ask the right questions.

It is sad really. People could be making so much more money if they just knew more money.

Remember the five kinds of equity that I mentioned above? Let's talk about each one.

Self-Equity

Money: Now remember, while you can use all of these equities on your job, what you should really be doing is finding some way to use them in a personal business. Your personal business can be big or small. It doesn't matter because the rules that govern building equity apply to all sorts of businesses. And start looking around! Listen to other people. Look for people who are doing what you would like to do, and for people who have what you would like to have and do what they do. Start reading books. Stop listening to people who are failing.

Bill: Money, I hate to interrupt you, but this seems kind of silly. Are you really saying that just listening to other people will build equity?

Money: Yes, money is simple. It only gets complicated because humans start getting all crazy about it.

Here's a good example. The next time someone says, "Would you be willing to look at a business that might help make you some extra money?" say "Yes!" It's that simple! But what most people do is immediately get suspicious and say "no."

When you invest in yourself—when you build self-equity, you will be amazed at how things will start to change for you.

It may not be very noticeable at first. But eventually, as you get better and better at being open to other opportunities and other perspectives, money will start to flow to you.

Bill: Wow, that's great stuff! I guess now I am glad I interrupted you. So would you please continue with the other equities?

Money: Of course.

Customer Equity

Money: If you want to make money, you have to have customers. Here is one thing that most humans don't understand. They don't understand that the only way money can be made is when one person (customer) buys something from another person (the seller). That's the only way money exchanges hands. Money goes where it is commanded to go. And the person who commands money to leave his/her pocket and go into someone else's pocket is called a customer.

Bill: Well Money, here I go again, interrupting you. But my readers are going to say, "I don't have a business. How could I have customers?" Can you help them out?

Money: Well that's a good point. But again, people don't think they have customers because they don't understand how money works.

Money is made when a customer gives up his/her money to someone else. That's it. So, if you have a business, your customers are the ones who give you money. But, remember, we also talked earlier about how your boss is your customer. You receive money for your work and value.

The real secret is to start thinking about anyone who gives you money as your customer. What do you do for a customer? You solve their problems. When you solve their problems, they give you their money.

Bill: Okay, so everyone has customers. It doesn't matter if you are an employee or entrepreneur. But what is customer equity?

Money: Customer equity is something you build. It is your list of customers. It is the people who are buying things from you. As you acquire customers, and keep them, this is a form of equity.

Suppose you are in a personal business. You have a product or service to sell. Your job is to go out and find customers who need and want this product. For example, suppose you have a product that will improve their health. Now, no one is looking for a product to "improve my health." They are looking for something that solves a problem. "Improving my health" is not a problem. But, "I don't have enough energy to get my work done in the afternoon" is a problem.

When you find a person with a problem that you can solve, you can turn them into a customer. You only have to do the work of building up your customer list one time.

Those customers will automatically reorder again and again. This is equity. That's what makes customer equity so powerful and so profitable.

Bill: How come people don't know this?

Money: Think about it. Who would have taught them this? Do you see now why self-equity is the first equity I talk about? You have to invest in self-equity in order to start making the fundamental changes that will allow you to learn more about money.

Bill: This is so exciting! Which equity is next?

Money: This next equity is extremely powerful: system equity. And again, it works whether you are an entrepreneur or an employee. But it is most powerful for entrepreneurs.

System Equity

Humans are always trying to "reinvent the wheel." They make everything more complicated than it has to be.

System equity is simple: it's plugging into an existing system. For example, many people start personal businesses with companies that already have a system. There are products, a system of keeping track of sales/customers, accountants, and shipping or service departments in place. This is extremely valuable stuff.

If you use your system, your system will make money for you. For example, your system might come with a personalized website for you. When you drive traffic to that website, people get the information they need about buying your services/products or in joining your company. That is huge, business-building equity.

Bill: Whoa, I love that. I think that the readers will already start to get some insight into the next equity: network equity. Do you have some great information for us about that?

Money: Of course! I am Money. When you build a network, Money notices!

Network Equity

Networks are made up of people. (Yes, there are computer networks, but these are part of system equity.) You build a network by getting people to join you in a common mission—to help everyone make more money.

If you want to build network equity fast, you have to let go of the ego traps. You want people in your network who are on fire because they also have a dream.

Now, a network is of very little value to you unless you make money on the work of the people who are in your network. In other words, you want to get paid not only for your work, but also for the work of the people who you bring into the business. Remember, you are building business builders.

Bill: Money, it's me again. I just love this, but I'm not sure that some of my readers are still following you. After all, we were taught to feel guilty about making money from other people. How does this work?

Money: You humans like to complicate everything, don't you? I guess when I told you that you have to let go of your "ego" I also forgot to tell you that you need to let go of your "craziness" as well!

I'll give you a specific example of how this works. Again, we'll be discussing this in other parts of this interview. So let's just keep it simple right now. There is a company out there that has a product or service that they want to sell to customers. They could set up a marketing channel with advertising and sales people. But that is expensive. Instead, they set up a business that creates networks of business builders. These business builders go out and find the customers and match them up with the company's products and services.

The company gives its agents and distributors two types of commissions: 1) straight commission for finding customers and 2) network commission for finding other agents and distributors. These other agents and distributors are also finding customers. This builds the company's sales quickly.

Now, it is easy to understand getting paid straight commission. Salespeople have been doing that for years. It is more difficult to understand that finding other agents and distributors (building a network) is even more important to the company. This is where the company gets leverage. Leveraging will skyrocket sales.

If you put yourself in the right circumstances, building a network will pay you more money than simply going out and selling a product or service. Why? You get paid not only for the work of the people you recruit; you get paid for the work of all the agents and distributors that they recruit! (Remember, no one gets any money unless sales are made to customers.)

Think about that person lying in the hammock. He did work hard, but he also built a network instead of doing the work on a one-to-one basis. Each of the people in that network was driven by his/her own dreams. So now, that guy is in his hammock and enjoying life. He has freedom because he has choices.

Mentor Equity

Bill: Money, I am looking at this last kind of equity: mentor equity. I have a feeling that kind of equity has something to do with the reason that guy can rest on the hammock and money is still flying off the wheel. Is that true?

Money: Yes, mentor equity is the most important kind of equity you can have.

Bill: But wait a second, didn't you say that self-equity is the most important kind of equity you have?

Money: Yes, but mentor equity is a type of self-equity. In fact, it is the ultimate sort of self-equity. You start with self-equity and end up with mentor equity. The mentor closes the circle.

Bill: What is mentor equity and why does it work so well?

Money: Mentor equity is getting paid for learning something and having a lot of people who are willing to teach you something.

There are a lot of people out there who are happy to charge you money to teach you something. Some of them are good and some are bad.

The best person to teach you about a subject is someone who has *actually done* what they are teaching you to do. This is mentor equity.

For example, would you like to learn how to fly an airplane? Who would be a better instructor—someone who read a book about flying or someone who has actually flown a plane? I'm not saying that the person who read the book about flying wouldn't be an inspiring teacher, but if that's who you learn to fly from, then please don't invite me on your next trip!

As you set out on the journey to make more money, you are going to run across many obstacles. The teachers will give you hints and clues about how to overcome the challenges.

But no matter how much help you get from other people, the most powerful learning you will experience is from experience itself. You will make mistakes. And if you succeed in your business, you are definitely going to be the kind of person who learned from those mistakes.

Over time, you will build mentor equity. You will become a very valuable animal. And, you will have value for other people. They will pay you to teach them what you know. If others can learn from your experiences, it saves them time and pain.

If you build a network company, you should get paid for your mentor equity. As you get promoted to higher levels within the company, you will receive bigger commissions, better bonuses, and other significant rewards. You will receive this compensation because your wealth of knowledge is building wealth in others.

Think about how this works. You start out with an investment in self-equity. Remember, your first step in building self-equity is to simply open yourself up to new ideas. This new awareness is going to send you on a journey. Along the journey you are going to pick up customer equity, system equity, network equity, and mentor equity. When you achieve true mentor equity, you have closed the circle. You now have a set of equities that will generate cash for you 24/7/366. (We say "366" because this even works in leap year!) If you want to make more money—close the circle.

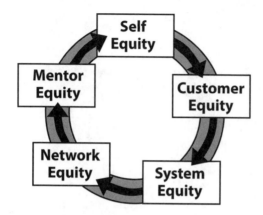

Bill: Money, that was extraordinary! Is that all there is to know?

Money: Well, you are human, so why not take a break? Let's start again on the next page.

Chapter 3
Your Job is Fixed Income!

Bill: Money, what do you say to people who think it is hard to live on a "fixed income"?

Money: I say that almost everyone in the world is living on a "fixed income." They just don't know it. The problem is, those fixed incomes can become "dashed" very quickly.

Bill: I'm not quite sure what you mean by someone's fixed income becoming "dashed" quickly. Can you explain this?

Money: Let's start with the many senior citizens who live on a fixed income—called Social Security. Each month they get a check. Supposedly, this is an annuity that they earned over their years of work.

Senior citizens complain because "I live on a fixed income." This means that they cannot make any more money each month. The seniors say, "Sometimes, my expenses are greater in a month that I budgeted for. My heater broke down and I had to pay $2000 to have it fixed." Let's face it, this is a problem.

Bill: Okay Money. We all know that Social Security is difficult to live on. But, I had the feeling that isn't what you really want to tell me here. What's this very dangerous warning you want to give us?

Money: Get ready! This is big, big, big!

If you have a job, you are living on a fixed income.

Let's face it, you go to work, you get paid, and it is the same amount you got last paycheck. By anyone's definition, isn't this a "fixed income"? I mean if you get the same amount of money each week, no matter how hard you work, isn't that a fixed income?

So why aren't people who have jobs saying, "It sure is difficult to live on a fixed income?" What if these people have an emergency? It is my observation that most people who have jobs also have mortgages, car loans, student loans, grocery bills, and other expenses each month that are very close to the amount of money they are taking home. Senior citizens who are living on a fixed income lower their expenses to meet the amount of money they are getting each month. Most non-senior citizens do not. They continue to get new cars, school loans, and borrow money from their home equity.

But that is not the dangerous part. I want every human to pay particular attention to this next sentence.

The real danger in having a fixed income that is not based on Social Security is that the income can become "dashed" unexpectedly and dramatically!

Did you get that? Do you see the danger? If you have a job, your fixed income could all become dashed in one phone call or one email from your boss. What happens then? If you have a single source of income, especially one that is fixed, you could be in big trouble—in an instant.

Take any 25-year period of economic history and there are going to be at least two recessions or bubble bursts. And when that happens, jobs are lost.

It doesn't have to be a recession. You may get fired. Your boss may discover that his favorite nephew is out of work—and that nephew gets your job! Maybe the owner of your company gets caught stealing. Perhaps there is a technology change and all of a sudden the industry you work in is gone. What happens to your fixed income then? It becomes "dashed"!

And, unlike the senior citizens who have full confidence that their Social Security payments (even though they are small) will come in month after month, anyone who has a job has no way of knowing that their fixed income check will be there at the end of the next pay period.

Yet, most job holders expect to keep their jobs. In fact, they expect to get periodic raises. (It is these "raises" that they think mean that their income is not fixed.) Every time they get a raise they buy something new—on credit. They think, "Well, I'll just use the raise this month to pay off that credit card." Or "I'll take out a loan and use the raise to pay for the monthly payments." So, when their "fixed income" job becomes a "dashed fixed income," layoff or firing, they are in real trouble.

Bill: Wait a minute, Money, what about overtime? Doesn't that make a person's income something other than fixed income?

Money: How many hours of overtime can you work each week? And you are still trading your time for dollars—a fixed income.

If you are a salaried employee, your income is also fixed. No matter how much (or how little) you work each week, your salary is fixed at a certain amount. "But what about bonuses?" you are asking. "Where I work, we can earn up to 10% of our salary in bonuses!"

Okay, that's great, but your income is still fixed.

"Oh no," the salespeople are shouting. "I am a salesperson. I get commissions. I'm not on a fixed income!"

Yes you are.

Bill: But isn't the chance for extra income the whole purpose of being a salesperson?

Money: Yeah, a lot of people think this way—especially salespeople. But let's face it, you can only earn so much.

Here is the problem. Sales people have quotas. These are generally adjustable and they never adjust down. If a sales person has a great month or a great year, this means the quota is raised the next year. What does this do? In many cases it reduces the amount of commissions you get on any sales that fall below the quota.

There are many cases of salespeople who get their commission percentage reduced because "they were making too much money." What this really means is that they were making more money than the sales manager (or some other boss) was making. And, perhaps their territory was cut in half.

Bill: Money, what does all this mean? I can see how dangerous it is for people to believe that they are not living on fixed incomes, but what do you suggest?

Money: Any human in their right mind will create a second source of income.

Bill: Are you saying that people should have a second job?

Money: No, they need a source of entrepreneurial income.

Having a second job doesn't protect you against fixed income, recessions, and bubble bursts. If your first job can become un-fixed, why can't the same thing happen to your second job?

Bill: Okay, a second job isn't the answer. So should people start saving money or investing it in the stock market?

Money: That's great—until it isn't! When a recession hits or a bubble bursts, whole industries end up in trouble. If you have your money in the stock market, what happens when there is a huge recession? Even if you have your investment diversified, a recession can wreck your entire portfolio.

Let's take an example. Let's say that real estate prices go into a sharp decline after going up year after year. This is an example of bubble bursting. All the sudden, people have mortgages that are higher than the value of their homes. They can no longer borrow money against their homes. If they have to sell their home (for a move, to pay off loans, or for any other reason) they end up in real trouble.

But it isn't just the real estate industry that's in trouble. As people have less money, they stop spending it on non-essential items like new cars. This causes a ripple effect and more and more industries begin to have difficulties.

Let's say you have a diversified portfolio—you have investments in precious metals and banks and pharmaceuticals and other types of industries. What is safe? Okay, maybe the price of gold starts to shoot up and you make money on that investment, but what about all the other investments?

You see, the same things that make depending on a job a risky business also make depending on your investments a risky business. (That's why they call it risk!)

Bill: Money, I know you aren't saying that people shouldn't invest in the stock market, right?

Money: No, I'm not saying that. Investing is a good idea. But every investment has risk and in a recession or a bubble-burst, you can lose a lot of money.

Bill: So what is the answer? Are there any investments you can make that are safe, and that will always give you a good return?

Money: Absolutely! You can invest in yourself!

Invest in Yourself

Money: Look, life is a journey. You humans are blessed with a life. The problem is, too many people try to go through that life—go on that journey—without making investments in themselves. In the United States, everyone goes to grade school and at least some high school. Most people finish high school and many people go on to college.

Now, I have some definite criticisms about the effectiveness of American education in terms of preparing people to generate money, but let's save that for later. Instead, let's assume that the things you learn in school really are worthwhile in terms of attracting and keeping money.

How much of an investment do most people make in themselves? The sad answer is that almost no one makes any investment after parents or society stop paying for it. They finish high school, or go to college, and that's it.

Bill: No wonder no one has ever really talked to you before Money. You are tough! I think you just told me that almost no one makes an investment in themselves—unless someone else is paying for it. Is that right?

Money: That's exactly what I am saying. But it isn't just my opinion. I think it is backed up by some very observable facts. Let's look at a typical person.

Joe comes from a middle-class family. He graduates college with a philosophy degree and takes 2½ years to find a good job. Joe spends the next 40 years working for various companies, gets laid off twice, hired somewhere else, has money taken out of his paycheck and put in his 401(k). Some years his retirement account is great, but every now and then it gets "smacked down" during a recession or bubble-bursting. But Joe hangs in there. He works hard. He has a couple of kids and passes along this lesson: "Get a good education and get a good job. Work hard and do your best. Try to get raises whenever you can. Invest your money wisely."

When was the last time Joe invested in himself during this lifetime? Was it the day he graduated from college? The answer is—probably.

But you know what is even worse? He passed those lessons on to his children. What did Joe tell them to do? His first bit of advice was "get a good education." But Joe's college major meant 2½ years searching for a job.

And what about later? Joe got laid off twice but he "stuck with it" in the same industry. How much sense does that make? And Joe's retirement strategy was turned over entirely to someone else. How much did that cost him? And how well did his investments do?

The problem with Joe—and with almost all people—is that he stopped learning the minute he walked out of college. Instead of investing in himself, he chose to simply "stick with it" no matter what happened.

Bill: Money, aren't you being hard on Joe? After all, he was a good citizen. He worked hard and did what he was told. He raised his children to respect the law and to be good citizens. He was smart. He saved money and invested. Why are you criticizing him?

Money: Money doesn't criticize people. Money only states facts. Joe put his future in the hands of other people. Over his lifetime, he could have made a lot more money. Isn't that why you are here interviewing me? Don't you want the straight facts?

Bill: You are right Money. This is too important to let emotions take over. You are saying that Joe should invest in himself. Can you tell us what you think Joe should have done?

Money: Joe should have asked a lot of questions. And he should have made an investment in himself. Joe could have learned about me.

But, almost no one today is taught the true facts about money. Instead, they just accept what they are told. They invest in a college education, their career, the stock market—but, they don't invest in themselves.

The question Joe should have asked is, "What do I need to do in order to make money?"

Bill: I see your point. I have to admit that it baffles me that people don't ask the simplest questions—even in the face of great evidence. Do you think it is a matter of luck?

Money: Well, I hate to admit it, but sometimes it is a matter of luck. For example, how many people will get "lucky" when they read this book? How many people will get "lucky" when a friend—or maybe even a stranger—just happens to ask them the right question at the right time?

Bill: I know that most of the people who are reading this book had some sort of "lucky" moment in their lives. It happened to me. And, I know the exact question that a young man asked me, and it changed my life. Can you guess what it was?

Money: Bill, I know exactly what that question was. You see, the minute that young man asked you that question, you got put on my list. The question was "Bill, what do you really want in life?"

You were a successful person by all accounts, right? You were 41 years old and a respected college professor. You had worked hard to earn your doctorate degree, and you were working hard as a professor—having a great impact on the lives of your students. But, you certainly were not getting rich. You were doing all the "right" things, but there was no way that you would end up with a lot of money in your life.

But then you got a call one evening from the husband of one of your students. He was only 21 years old. Why did this young man, who was 20 years younger than you, ask you to change your life? It's simple, he was building a business and wanted you to get involved.

Bill: I certainly remember my response. It was "How do I know what I want in life? No one ever asked me that question before, so I never thought about it!"

I also told him, "This is one of those crazy business schemes and you are going to lose all your friends by calling them on the phone and asking them questions like that."

Money: But you were lucky. You ran into someone who was brave enough to ask a question that shut you up. It took a while, but it changed you, didn't it?

Bill: Yes it did. I wanted nothing to do with what this young man was offering, but over the next few months that simple question really began to eat at me. It made me question all the basic facts of my life.

Money: Yes, that's exactly the point. You hadn't asked yourself "What do I really want out of life?" And even when those recessions hit, or the bubble bursts, or when the boss fires you, if you haven't asked yourself that one basic question, you will never learn to invest in yourself.

Bill: None of my bosses had ever asked me that question. They were always too busy telling me what they wanted me to do. In fact, they were very good at telling me what they wanted me to do.

About six months after the young man asked that question, we were sitting on the beach, and I noticed them using some products that I had never seen in the stores. I asked him, "Are they from your business?", and he told me that they were. My next question was so outrageously rude that I can't believe I asked it. "How much are you making every month on that business?" I asked.

Why is that question so rude? I would never ask that question about someone's job. Can you imagine walking up to one of your friends and saying "How much money do you make on the job?" It just isn't done.

The answer he gave me was straightforward and honest. And that answer changed my life forever. Money, you probably already know what the answer was, but I think it will surprise the readers of this book when they learned just how little it was. He told me, "Bill, we are making about $400 a month on this business."

$400 a month! That isn't a lot of money. I made far more than that on my job. But just learning that someone could create an income stream on their own—without having a job—told me something very important. It told me that money could be made in a whole different way. It is alerted me to the fact that I had stopped thinking, and stopped asking questions. Learning that someone who was barely old enough to vote was able to generate $400 out of thin air was a revelation. And, the fact that he did it month after month was even more surprising. I had to know more.

Money Talks about the List

Money: That was the second time you showed up on my list Bill. It was a big day. But you see, it wasn't just that you were lucky enough to have a brave friend approach you, you also decided to take the question seriously and start investing in yourself. Not many people do that.

Bill: Okay Money—there you go with that "list" again. Before we go any farther, I have to understand more. What do you mean that I was on your list for the second time?

Money: Well, this is supposed to be a secret, but since you went to all this trouble to interview me, I will share that secret with you right now. If more humans knew about the "list" maybe they would have more money and lead more fulfilling lives.

Every day, Money gets a list. After all, I have to be ready to go where I am commanded to go. I want to make sure that when someone says "Money, go to Bill," I am ready to rush right into your arms!

So I get a list of all the people who just started making an investment in themselves. When that young man called, you had an opportunity to make an investment in yourself. If you had done it that night, I would have been ready.

Now, it took you about six months to really make the changes necessary in order to start making more money. Opportunity knocked again.

Bill: There is a list? You gotta be kidding!

Money: No, I'm not kidding. It isn't hard to keep a list. There aren't many people on it—less than 1% of people in the world. But only a very small percentage of those people stick with it, and make a lot of money. The people who succeed have a reason to succeed. There is something that drives them.

Bill, you are lucky. That guy asked, "What do you really want out of life?" And he phrased the question just right. If he had said to you, "I have a new business I want to tell you about," it would not have had the same impact. He set you up for success. He set you up for success because he asked you a question that mattered. The way he asked that question was the "difference that made a difference."

Bill: My life is entirely different because of that one question.

Money: But Bill, the luck only ran as far as you being contacted and asked the question. After that, it all depended upon you making the investment in yourself. You started looking around you for new opportunities and made some serious changes in the way you think. You spent time, and you spent some money. You began to grow as a human. All that was part of your investment in yourself.

Bill: Yeah that was tough. I remember thinking to myself "How is it that I'm the only one who sees this?" The people I worked with didn't see it. Some of my friends didn't see it. Members of my family didn't see it. When they looked at me, they saw a successful person—a college professor with a good income, a nice home and a bright future. And yes, it was good. But the fact is, once Ron Browning asked me that question, I realized I wanted more.

Money: I was wondering if you're going to tell everyone his name. He was definitely on my list. In fact, he had a star next to his name!

Bill: (Laughing) I guess he did! That was one brave guy. And he didn't stop there. He built a very successful business and helped a lot of people on the way. Ron and his wife Sharon are such positive people. After building a big business as young people, they went on to create a really big traditional business. And they did all that because they took the time to ask some questions and make an investment in themselves. They taught me to do the same thing. I guess if you are going to have a list, I'd put them pretty close to the top.

Money: Well, you're the first one to know about the list. I imagine that almost everyone who reads this book is going to get on that list. Hopefully, they'll stay on the list as well.

Bill: Money, this is bringing back a lot of memories. Can we talk a little bit about exactly how people can make an investment in themselves?

Money: It might just be luck that brings you in contact with a person that opens your eyes, but when that person presents you with a different message, you have to be ready to listen.

Bill: Well Money, that's what happened to me when Ron called me. I shot him down with all the clichés that I could muster. But truthfully, I knew absolutely nothing about it.

Money: Bill, I have something to tell you. Did you know that I almost had to take your name off the list?

Bill: I bet. But when my wife Jeanne and I began to think about what we really wanted out of life, my whole world changed quickly. Again, it was Sharon and Ron who showed us how to do it. "Get specific," they told us. And once we got started, look out! We had a lot of dreams.

Money isn't drawn to your dream. Instead, it is your dream that drives you to do the things—the hard things—that you need to do in order to attract money.

I think this is an important distinction for everyone to understand. People have to remember that money only goes where it is directed to go. If a person wants more money, they need to have a reason to go out and get it.

I am going to make a statement now to all of my readers. I want you to pay attention to what I'm about to say, because it is really important. And, after my interview with Money, I'm even more convinced of how important it is.

If your dream is to "make more money" then you are cheating yourself and your family.

Do you know why? "Making more money" will never help you get through the challenges that are sure to stand in your way. However, if your dreams are things like "I want to have enough money so that I can be free from the demands that a job places on me," then you have something worth fighting for. Or, maybe your dream is "To have enough money to have my spouse quit her job and stay home with the baby." It can even be something much simpler such as "I'd like to have enough money to pay my bills each month so I can stop this terrible stress and worry." Some people might dream for a new car, or a boat, or more vacations.

The important thing is that you do not dream about "making money." Instead, you want to visualize how your life will change. You must visualize what money can do for you. During this interview,

Money will continue to tell you that he is just a tool. Money is a tool for humans to use to get what they want.

Money: Bill, even after that day on the beach, you still struggled for a while.

But the unique thing about you is that you not only learned how to make money, you began to write books that taught other people how to make more money. A lot of names have appeared on our list because people read your books. Sometimes they were intrigued by the title and bought the book, and sometimes someone gave them that book. That's why you got this interview with me. We know that you will take what I say seriously, and you won't try to disguise it or hide it in order to trick other people into doing what you want. Instead, we trust you to use this information to help other people.

Bill: That's right Money. And I do try to remind people that there are three things that are going to get in their way as they try to change their life and pursue their dreams: little problems, big problems, and other people.

When Jeanne and I decided to pursue our dreams, we faced all of these. We took them each one at a time. And we didn't let other people steal our dreams.

Don't be angry with them. Instead, just be nice to them. But for goodness sakes, don't listen to them!

Well, Money, this chapter has been about the human side, hasn't it? Now I think it is time for us to listen to you. I'm going to ask you some questions that people have been asking me.

Money: Sounds good Bill. I'm ready to give people the inside secrets about how money works.

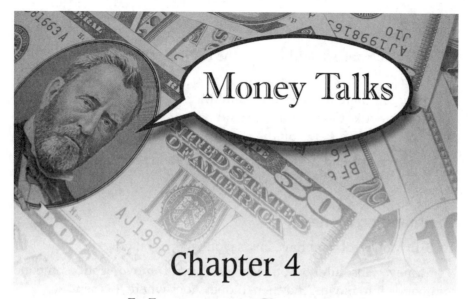

Money Talks

Chapter 4

Money Says: Command Me

Money is such a powerful force in our lives that we often forget that we are in charge. It is a tool. We are the only ones who can command money.

We are used to having a job where someone else tells us how much we can be paid. Our boss commands money to go to us, and how much should go to us. We don't get to decide that.

We turn over our investments to people called "brokers" (isn't it ironic that they are called brokers?). These days, we really aren't too involved with our money. It is no wonder that we don't understand how to get people to command their money to go to us.

Believe me, one of the most important things that you can learn is how to command other people to give you their money. All you have to do is give them a good reason. In this chapter, Money and I are going to begin to lay the foundations that you will need in order to get people to command their money to go to you. You are going to have to do some thinking, take a hard look at the realities, and make some tough decisions and changes.

However, there is great news, and Money is going to share it with you in this book. Keep an open mind as you read these pages. Don't get discouraged. Relief is on the way—and it is simple and powerful.

Money and I had a great conversation about command. Here are some very interesting excerpts below.

Commanding Money

Bill: Money, do you have any say in where you go?

Money: Absolutely not. Money doesn't move until someone commands it to move. And then, money goes where it is sent.

Bill: Who decides where money will go?

Money: Only the people who have the money can decide where it is to go.

Bill: Why would someone command money to go to someone else?

Money: There is only one reason. The person sending the money feels that she/he is getting something in return that is greater value than the money was.

Bill: Money, a lot of the people I speak to feel like their money is being taken from them. For example, in 2006 through 2008 millions of people invested in real estate and lost money when they got mortgages that they really couldn't afford.

Money: Yes, I watched that with great interest. But, the people who took on those crazy mortgages still commanded their money. They made the decision to send their money to the mortgage companies. They made the decision to spend their money on those houses.

Remember, money does not deal in fairness or ethics. Money is just a tool. There have always been people who try to sell things that other people really don't need, or to sell things that have lesser value than the money being charged.

The problem is that many humans do not understand how money is made, so they do not understand how to command money. For example, during the housing crisis, many people lost their homes because they had purchased a variable rate mortgage. When they first started making their payments, the interest rates on the mortgages were very low. However, they quickly rose, sometimes to very high levels. Soon, these people couldn't afford the payments. To complicate matters, there was a recession, and lots and lots of layoffs. Even people who made responsible money decisions on their mortgages forgot about the fact that they could be laid off.

Was it the fault of the unscrupulous lenders? Was it the fault of the uneducated buyers? Money does not have an opinion on that.

Bill: Well Money, I understand that as an inanimate object you do not have opinions on ethics. I am going to do my best not to use my personal feelings about this to condemn anyone. However, I will say that humans need to be better educated about money. If they understood things like risk and rewards, they could live far better lives. Hopefully, books like this will help people understand money and how it works.

How about when the government takes money through taxes? In a case like that, people aren't really commanding money to go to the government are they?

Money: Sorry Bill. Who do you think voted for those crazy politicians? And, how do you think those politicians stay in office?

In almost all political systems, politicians respond to two things— money and votes. Politicians need money in order to get reelected. They promise things to large donors.

This is politics. Don't be surprised. That's the way it works. When people vote for politicians, those politicians levy taxes. So yes, people actually do command their money to go to taxes because the people vote for the politicians who levy those taxes.

Money: There are still plenty of ways to make money and live a great life—despite taxes. Only you can set yourself and your family free.

Bill: Okay, what about dishonest people who steal money? In a case like that, no one commands their money to go to someone who is stealing from them. Am I right?

Money: Well, yes and no. Burglars and thieves do take money from people against their will. On the other hand, there are times when people command their money to go directly to the thieves. There are clever "white-collar" criminals who steal people's money by taking advantage of human nature frailties such as greed. How many people have invested their money into a sure-fire, just can't miss scheme, only to find out that they got ripped off?

Bill: White-collar criminals often prey on the least educated, most vulnerable people in our economy, right?

Money: Well, sometimes... but often, it is the people who have a lot of money to command that are the biggest victims of these schemes. If you have any doubts, watch "American Greed" on television, a true crime series that examines the dark side of the American dream. And don't forget the whole stock market crisis of 2008. How about all those stockbrokers who invested billions (albeit of other people's money) into high-risk portfolios that were chock full of mortgages that would never be paid off? Almost every single one of those people had college degrees—many of them from prestigious schools. Many had MBA's and other advanced degrees. What about all those people?

Bill: Stop, stop! This is terrible. You are taking away all our excuses.

Money: Basically, yes. In both those cases, humans commanded their money to go to the politicians, stockbrokers, speculators, and bad dealmakers. That's the only way money could have gone there.

Bill: By this time, anyone who is reading this book is probably lying on the floor crying. Is there any good news?

Money: There is only good news. In fact, it is fabulous news. The things you need to know in order to make money and keep it are so simple that it requires almost no effort to learn them. When you learn them, you will be amazed just how simple it is to apply them. When you apply them, you will always have money. When you always have money, you always have the ability to command it to do exactly what you want to do.

When you learn how to make money and keep it, you are far less likely to command money to do stupid things. Your power increases. Your stress is reduced. You gain your financial freedom.

Let me end with these thoughts. Humans, don't hide your head in the sand. Take a look around. There are millions of very wealthy people out there who are not any smarter than you are. They don't have any magic powers. They made their money the honest, easy way. If you want to be one of them, all you have to do is learn a few simple things. In fact, I'm going to share a seven-step process with you that is so easy and simple you might just laugh out loud when you read it.

If you want money, today is the perfect day to start getting it. Just learn a few facts, make a few adjustments, and start reeling in the cash. You are going to love it.

Money Talks

Chapter 5
Risk and Reward

During the many hours of conversation that I had with Money, the subject of risk and reward came up again and again. Money was clear on this matter: when you know how to make money, you reduce risk, and set yourself free. Money pointed out how understanding risk and reward is essential for understanding money and how it works.

Money said, " In some ways, risk and reward are opposites. Yet, they are so closely linked together that they are really the two platforms on which money-making and money-losing are balanced."

This is a very strong statement. And as I looked over my notes before writing this book, I decided that the subject was so important that it required its own chapter. After speaking so long with Money, I feel qualified to explain risk and reward to you. However, I am going to use Money's own words to help carry the message home.

On the other hand, many of our laws and social policies completely ignore the impact of risk and reward. While Money did have something to say about this, I will, whenever necessary, interject my own interpretations of how governments, politicians, and other groups get the risk and reward partnership so utterly mixed up. Remember, I am not doing this to further a political program. In fact, like Money, I am going to urge you to stay out of political discussions. Understanding risk and reward as it actually works is essential to your success. Don't get caught up with politicians who are using their own version of risk and reward to distract you from the most important money-related issue: your own personal financial freedom.

Risk and Reward

Bill: Money, we seem to keep coming back to two important concepts—risk and reward. Can you help define risk and reward for our readers?

Money: Sure!

Risk

Risk occurs whenever there is a danger that something will be lost. Of course, in order to lose something, you must first possess it. When people make an investment, they incur risk. There are many things that people can risk. For example, they can risk their reputations, their lives, their security, and their money. Bill, you risked your reputation, your time, and your money in order to write this book, didn't you?

Bill: That's right Money. It took me a long time to track you down. Some of my friends said I was crazy.

Money: And even after you made the decision to come look for me, despite the taunts and ridicule of some people, you still didn't know if it would be a waste of time. And, when you had the interview, you still had to give up a lot of time to write this book, and then pay someone to do the editing, cover design, printing, etc. You spent time and money without ever knowing if you would make money from the effort. This is risk.

Bill: Well, anyone who is in business for themselves takes risk. But, that's the nature of business, isn't it?

Money: Yes, that's exactly the nature of business. When someone starts a business, they put themselves at risk. No one ever knows if a business is going to work out. For example, you might think that you have identified a problem, that you have identified the people who have that problem, and you may even have a product or service that you think these people will buy to solve that problem. But, you never know until the transaction is done. This is risk.

Bill: Money, there is a famous story about a philosophy professor who gave a test with one question on it. All his students were seated in the class waiting for the test. They had the traditional "blue books" for writing their answers to the questions they expected. But once the test was passed out, there was just one question; "What is risk?"

All of the students began to write long answers about risk. They dredged up all the information they could remember. But one student was finished the test in about two minutes. When he got the question, "what is risk?" he quickly jotted down four words, turned in his blue book, and left the class. The other students all thought he was crazy. Many of his friends assumed that he had not studied for the test and had just given up.

Money: I heard the story Bill, and I love it. What were the four words that the student wrote on his test?

Bill: He simply wrote in his test booklet, "This is a risk." The professor gave him an A+.

Money: That is a great example of risk. He took a chance that he might lose something. If the professor did not like his answer, he would've received a failing grade in the final exam, and quite possibly a failing grade for the class. If his parents were paying for his education, there could've been some real trouble! This is risk.

Reward

Money: Of course, the student in the example above took the risk in order to gain the rewards. Remember, he received an A+ grade from the professor. If that student had done the same thing as everyone else, his boldness would not have stood out. It would have been difficult to distinguish his answer from all the others. But, because he was clever, and because he solved a problem for that professor, he received the top reward the professor could give him.

Bill: What do you mean he "solved a problem for the professor"? How did he solve the professor's problem? Didn't the professor give the students the problem?

Money: Think about it for a second. That student treated his professor as his customer. Customers are people with a problem who can give you a reward. Now in most cases, we think of the reward our customers are going to give us in terms of money. But, there are many other kinds of rewards.

Bill: Money, I am still not sure what problem this professor had. And I am sure that most of my readers don't get it either.

Money: Okay, let's look at this closely. Now some of your readers are probably thinking that we are wasting our time talking about this. But there is a lesson here: the lesson is to understand how to delight your customers and separate yourself from the competition. You can only do this by taking a risk. There is no other way to do it. Yet, if you take that risk, and it ends up delighting your customers, you get the biggest rewards. If you are looking for money, then you will get a lot of it. But no matter what the rewards are, taking a risk that the delights your customers will produce the biggest rewards.

This professor teaches the same course semester after semester. He teaches philosophy. He loves philosophy but let's face it, most of his students do not. What is his problem? He gets bored. He is looking for someone who really "gets it" when it comes to philosophy. He wants to be delighted. He reads those papers semester after semester and sees the same old thing. His students are dredging up all the facts they can think of and throwing them on the paper.

But then, here comes someone who surprises him. Here comes a young man who separates himself from the competition by taking a risk. He challenges that philosophy professor and quite literally says to him, "I dare you not to accept this." What does the professor think? He thinks, "Finally, I got through to someone." He is delighted, and he is delighted to be able to reward that student with an A+.

Bill: Wow Money. I think I just "got it." And, I think I can see why so many people are afraid to take a risk. This could be one of the most important points that you and I have uncovered. I mean it, this is big, big, big. Would you mind if I took over for a few minutes and speak directly to my readers?

Money: No, in fact I would be delighted.

Bill: Readers, take note. There are so many great lessons here. As Money was talking, my head was spinning. Let's talk about this money risk/reward paradigm more closely, because this can really help you make money.

Over the years, I have observed how people are afraid to take risk. Oh, when they get a new idea, they are all excited about it. They might even throw some time and money behind their idea. But, at the first sign of an obstacle their whole system collapses. The first time a friend says to them, "What are you doing? Are you crazy? What will people think about you?", they simply give up.

I have noticed that people are much more willing to risk time and money than risk their reputations. Maybe that's because time and money don't talk back to you. Time and money don't spread rumors about you. Time and money don't make fun of you. But, your friends, families, neighbors and associates are different. It seems like they never hesitate to point out your mistakes, or to question your decisions. They love to play the "I told you so" game, don't they? But you have to understand something, as it is fundamental to your success. I want you to read the following statement at least three times.

When you do something out of the ordinary, like take a risk in order to get big rewards, you aren't just putting yourself at risk. You are putting everyone around you at risk. If you make some changes in your life and start getting more than everyone else, this puts them at risk.

They don't want you to challenge the status quo. They don't want you to grow and change. They want you to be just like them. If you do something different and it brings you great success, they might see themselves "losing" the things that you gained. This is a risk, and many of your friends, families, neighbors, and work associates will try to get you to stop doing this "crazy new thing" so that they can remain in their comfort zones. Their beliefs are in doubt, because you did something different.

Risk Without Reward

Bill (continued): Let's be clear, when you decide to assume some risk, you do it with some reward in mind. Let's say you invest some money in the stock market. The reward that you expect is that the value of the stocks will go up. If you start your own business, it is because you want the rewards that you will get from being successful. Not only will you receive money, but also you will be able to work for yourself. You are the boss. That can be very rewarding.

If you take a risk on your job, you also expect rewards. Maybe you come up with a way to cut costs and increase sales. You write a report, on your own, and make a presentation to your boss and other executives. If they like what they see, they might reward your initiative by giving you a promotion or a raise.

If your risk/reward behavior disturbs the comfort zone of those around you, you are putting them at risk—and they don't see any rewards. Can you imagine how dangerous this is for them? Can you imagine how much this disturbs them? So, don't be surprised when they say things like, "Are you crazy? That's not how people like us behave. Stop trying to be so different from us."

When You Take Risk, Your Customers Get the Rewards

Money: Bill, I'd like to explain the concept of "when you take risks, your customers get the rewards." As you said, "This is big, big, big!" (Bill, you are having an influence on me! I never said anything like "big, big, big" before.)

When you decide to take on some risk in order to get rewards, you want to add value for your customers. When you add value to your customers, they get a reward. They get the value. If you are solving a problem for them, they get the solution to the problem. When you solve their problems, you do something very important for them. You reduce their risk.

You reduce their risk! Can you imagine how important that is? Your friends, family, and associates had their risk increased when you decided to seek rewards. But, your customers actually have their risks reduced when you seek rewards by solving their problems. And, here is something very important to know. Every time you reduce a customer's risk, they give you money.

Let me give you an example from a relatively new company that is operating in the United States. It is a new kind of taxicab service called Uber. This business is exploding because it reduces risk and solves problems. The risk that Uber has solved for the customers is that their taxicab will not show up.

You see, when the founders of Uber created their company, they saw a big problem—and people with money. When you are out on the town and don't have a car, you need transportation. When you are going to the airport and don't want to leave your car in the parking lot, you need transportation. And, you need this transportation to be timely and reliable. These are your problems.

But, when you use an ordinary taxicab, you also have risk. For example, if you are going to a show at a theater and want to go to dinner afterwards, you run the risk that you will not be able to find a taxicab when the show lets out. Hundreds of people are coming out of the show at the exact same time as you—and all of them are looking for taxicabs as well. That is a risk.

The solution to the customer's problem (using a taxicab instead of driving a car) works—but not all the time. But, when you use Uber, the ride service is scheduled just for you. You can order it on your smart phone. The driver is looking for you. You can track your driver on your phone. This reduces your risk. You gladly give them money in exchange for the service. And, you will gladly choose them over a taxicab because it reduces your risk. In other words, by reducing risk, Uber stands out over the competition.

Reduce your customers' risks and they will give you money. This works no matter who your customers are. Is your boss a customer on your job? Certainly! Your boss has risks. Her boss set goals and objectives. If she doesn't reach those goals, she might be fired. But she can't reach those goals on her own. She is depending on you and your teammates. If you "step out of the crowd" and do something extraordinary, you reduce her risks, which is exactly what she wants.

Always remember: when you take risks, both you and your customers can earn rewards! But, when you take risks, you will always increase somebody's risks—and they may not be getting rewards.

Bill: Money, that is stupendous! Every person in the world needs to understand this. This is such a key element to making money. So, we want to undertake risk in order to get rewards.

Money: That's exactly right Bill. Remember, we talked earlier about when you work for someone else, you think you are giving up risks (and to some degree you are) and you know you are giving up some rewards. And, on the face of it, it makes sense. A steady paycheck is much less risky than being an entrepreneur.

But, if you're laid off, the company has a bad year, or the boss wants to hire her nephew and replace you—suddenly your "steady" paycheck is at risk.

Bill: But Money, what are we humans to do? Do you have some advice that doesn't require a great deal of risk? And, do you have some advice that can bring some excellent rewards?

Money: Absolutely!

Today, everyone should be looking at a new kind of paradigm for making money. This new paradigm reduces risk and maximizes rewards. I call it the Financial Freedom Hybrid.

It's simple.

1. Learn the Seven Secret Steps for making money. It is essential that people understand that these steps apply to both jobs and personal businesses.

2. Then determine how to create low-risk equity. And, you do this at the same time you have a job. In other words, you are using your job as salary, and you are creating a business for yourself "on the side" that utilizes built-in equity to generate low-risk, high-reward returns. That's why I call it a Financial Freedom Hybrid.

Bill: How can people do that? I get the "job" part. Everyone gets that. But what are the low-risk, high-reward ventures that are out there for people?

Money: My seven secret steps for making money will help you find these ventures. There are absolutely hundreds of thousands of companies out there who have a product or service that will solve the problem for people.

Best of all, in today's technology-driven environment, you can set these businesses up to bring you long-lasting, repeating sources of income.

Anyone who wants to have a business "on the side" can partner with these companies and help connect them with customers. Customers love it because they are getting added value. In addition, they are working with someone they know, like, and trust. This reduces the risk. Remember, when you accept risk and get rewards, the customer has reduced her/his risks.

Go back to the chapter on "The 5 Kinds of Equity" and review that material. Now imagine this: you have a job, but you haven't fooled yourself into thinking that this job is going to be around forever and that it will pay for your comfortable retirement. In other words, be honest with yourself about the risks in your job. Then find a way to bring suppliers and customers together. Add value to this chain, and sell that value to the customers. Or, add value to the chain and sell that value back to the suppliers.

Now, your low-risk, high-return business builds and builds over time. When it comes time for you to retire (and maybe that's much earlier in life) you have a source of income other than Social Security. Before retirement, you can use that extra income to invest in more equity. Or, you can use that money to enjoy your time off. You decide.

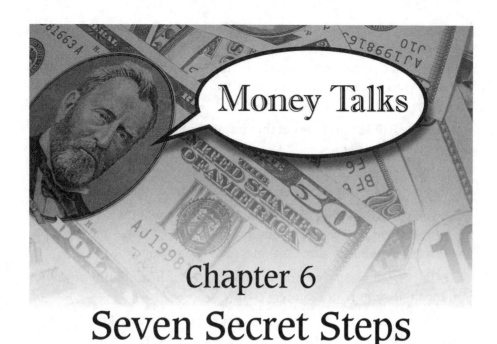

Money Talks

Chapter 6
Seven Secret Steps

How To Make Money

In this section, I am going to give you Money's formula for making money. Now let's think about this for a second. If you want to know how to make more money—and keep it—is there anywhere else that would be better to go than to Money itself? After all, who knows more about making money than Money?

For many of you, this will be the most valuable part of this book. In fact, it might just be the topic that you were thinking of when you heard that I had interviewed Money. When many of my friends, family, and readers learned that I was going to ask Money questions, they said things to me like, "Would you ask Money how I can make more money?" Well, here it is, straight from Money's mouth!

Bill: Money, there is one question that an overwhelming majority of people want me to ask you. It is "How can I make more money?" Are you ready to answer that question?

Money: Not yet.

Bill: What you mean not yet? I traveled all this way to find you and now you're telling me I have to wait to ask the most important question that my readers want answered? Do you think that's fair?

Money: Fair? Didn't we get that point straightened out yet? Money doesn't care about fair.

Bill: Okay, okay. I have to keep remembering that you are Money and not a human. But come on, can't we just get to the point?

Money: Aha! Getting to the point is exactly what I want to do. But you asked the question the wrong way. And, that is how most people ask this particular question. You included the wrong word.

Bill: Let me look back on my notes to see if I can figure out what you mean. It's the word "more," right?

Money: Yep, there is no "more" about it. You either know how to make money or you do not.

Bill: I got it. Let's try it again. "Money, how can I make money?"

Money: That is the million-dollar question. This is going to take some time to answer, so sit back and relax. But when I have finished, you and your readers will know the seven simple secrets to making money. All you have to do to make money is to repeat the seven simple secrets again and again.

Bill: Okay Money, let's get started!

How To Make Money: Follow Seven Secret Steps

Money: Here is how we are going to go about this. I am going to give you the Seven Secret Steps for making money, and then go over each one of them. However, I'm going to explain #4, "Add Value to the Solution" in greater detail. This step is a common stumbling block for many people. (Bill, maybe you can write a separate chapter about this topic.)

So let's look at the seven steps. I call them "secret" because that is exactly what they appear to be. Yet, if you understand money and people, there is no reason for these seven steps to be mysterious!

The Seven Secret Steps for making money are:
1. **Find a big problem**
2. **Determine if the people who have that problem also have money (these are your customers)**
3. **Identify a solution for the problem that your customers face (Don't reinvent the wheel)**
4. **Add value to the solution**
5. **Intercept the people with the pain and STIR that pain**
6. **Trade your solution to the pain for money**
7. **Relentlessly repeat steps 1 through 6**

Bill: Money, would you mind if I try to summarize our conversation about the Seven Secret Steps?

Money: That's a great idea! Go for it.

Bill: Okay, here goes.

1. **Find a big problem** – There are a lot of problems in the world. The giant hamburger chain McDonald's found a problem—people didn't have enough time to get something to eat. They offered walk-up service and later, the drive-through window. Amazon found that people who love to read didn't have the time to go to the bookstores. They created the Kindle. Find people with problems, and follow Money's example. Look for problems on both ends of the value added chain. Find suppliers who need help getting their products into the hands of paying customers, and find paying customers who need products and services.

2. **Determine if the people who have that problem also have money (these are your customers)** – Remember what Money said about customers—they are people with money, your money! It doesn't do you any good to solve problems for people who do not have money. Your buyers don't have to be rich; they just have to be able to afford your product or service. No one would accuse people who eat McDonald's hamburgers as being rich. Yet, by focusing on a mass-market, with huge demand, and providing a fast, efficient service, McDonald's has made a fortune. And, wouldn't you like to have a penny for everyone who made an additional purchase when the drive-through cashier at McDonald's asks, "Would you like fries with that? "

3. **Identify a solution for the problem that your customers face (Don't reinvent the wheel)** – Money would like to make a huge point here. Money gave me this interview to help ordinary men and women. This means that Money thinks that you should not become a manufacturer. You should not open up a huge, expensive storefront. Instead, you should simply become the person who brings sellers (suppliers) and customers (buyers) together. Remember, both the suppliers and the customers have problems. You make your money by being the solver of the problems for both ends of the added value chain. This reduces your risk and your need for cash investment. Yet, if you do it right, your ability to make money is unlimited.

4. **Add value to the solution** – Money will be discussing this in greater length in the next chapter, as adding value is one of the biggest obstacles in making money. You *must* have confidence in yourself, and you must know what is valuable to others. People try to make money without the concept of value. This will kill you every time. But don't worry, Money will show you just how to find that value.

5. **Intercept the people with the pain and STIR that pain** – This is a critical point. Money says that most humans just don't know how to do this. It isn't surprising to Money, because humans are very seldom taught how to do this. What does it mean to "intercept" customers? You have to be there when they are looking for a solution to the problem. And what does it mean to "stir the pain"? Well, you need to first make sure that your customers feel the pain of not having what they want. And then you need to ask them questions, show them happy

people who are solving their problems by using your products, share stories about how people are living better lives because they use your products, etc. You want to introduce your solution to their pain! The more they want your solution, the more likely they are to buy.

6. **Trade your solution to the pain for money** – Again, here is a critical place where humans have difficulty. They have difficulty accepting money for relieving pain. You must be sure to always get paid when you solve someone's problems. And hey, don't forget the McDonald's hamburger question that every server asks—"would you like fries with that?" If you are solving their problem with one product, think how much less pain they will have—and how much happier they will be—if they buy more products from you.

7. **Relentlessly repeat steps 1 through 6** – Do we really need to say more? If you make money by following steps one through six, why would you possibly not do it again and again? Be relentless. Look for more opportunities. Find more people with problems, stir their pain and sell them a solution.

Follow the Seven Secret Steps until they are no longer secret. Share them with others. You are in a position to relieve the pain of thousands of people. You are in the business of connecting customers to suppliers, and you are in the business of building business builders. What could be more satisfying than that?

Look, you can work and work and work. You can create a factory. You can build a huge retail outlet. Or, you can bring customers and buyers together. That is why Money likes to say, "Build a tollbooth—not a toil booth." Build the roads and networks that connect customers and suppliers. Make a little bit on each transaction. Build a group of other tollbooth operators. Teach them how to do the same thing.

Remember, money has a flow. Every time you make that flow faster and easier, you make money.

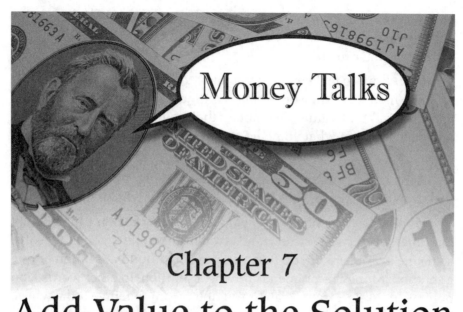

Chapter 7
Add Value to the Solution

Now you know the 7 secret steps. Pretty easy, right?

With that in mind, Money is about to give you some information about #4—Adding Value to the Solution. Most people have absolutely no idea how to add value to each and everything they do. Yet, adding value is the true key to making money.

A note from Bill: At this point, money took out a piece of paper with a very simple drawing on it. You can see that drawing below.

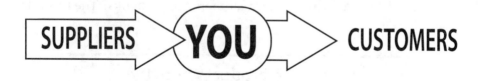

Money: Take a look at this drawing. It is quite simple, yet it is one of the most powerful moneymaking tools you will ever come across. In fact, it is the absolute basis for the entire moneymaking process. If people want to know how to make money, the very first thing they must understand is how to add value.

Here is the reason why:

If you want to make money, you must sell something. And in order to make money selling something, you must add value to something and then sell that value. The money that you charge your customers will be the total of what you paid for your supplies plus the value you add.

Okay, let's get started on this. This is big, big, big. Take a look at that drawing again, and see if you can figure out what it means.

Suppliers—remember, you want to be busy making money, not building products, services, and systems. You are going to solve someone's problems. To do this, you can either build a solution or buy a solution. Money recommends buying a solution. In other words, you don't want to start from scratch. You don't want to reinvent the wheel. If someone has a solution to a problem already, just buy that solution from them and sell it to the customers. (Adding some value of your own along the way.)

Let me give you an example: Amazon. When Amazon was first developed, they had no products of their own. Amazon saw people with a problem. People liked to read books, but they wanted a more convenient way to get those books. Amazon found suppliers like authors and publishers who already had books. The publishers and authors who already had books are the "suppliers" (at least for this example).

Amazon bought the books from these people and then ADDED VALUE to them. Amazon then sold the books to their customers. How much could Amazon charge the customers for the books? The formula is simple:

Cost of the products from the suppliers + the added value
= selling price to customers.

Humans, that is it! That is the only way to make money. Well, it is the only way to make money honestly. (Bill, I'm assuming that all the readers of your book want to make money honestly and ethically.)

Bill: Money, I think that most of my readers are going to understand the "suppliers and customers concept" but they may not yet get the "adding value" concept. How about giving us some examples of how Amazon adds value?

Money: Good point. Here we go.

Nothing has value unless the customers perceive and believe the value. Value is never in the seller's mind. Value is only in the mind of the customer.

First, I will give you some examples of how Amazon adds value, and then I will talk about the perception of value.

Okay, what does Amazon do to add value? For the moment, let's talk only about the printed books that Amazon sells. Amazon is interested in people who like to read books. They are more likely to use Amazon again and again.

So Amazon created an easy-to-use platform for these readers. This has great added value. It's easy to shop from home, credit cards are accepted, reader reviews are posted, and customers can search for a particular type of book.

Amazon has become the largest retailer in the world for a very specific reason. They add value for their customers.

Finally, Amazon knows they have two kinds of customers. They have readers and they have authors/publishers. You see, Amazon adds value towards both ends of the adding value chain. They give their readers *all* the added values we described above. But, they also give their suppliers (authors/publishers) value as well. Amazon recognizes that the authors and publishers are not just Amazon suppliers. No, the authors/publishers are also Amazon's customers. Amazon adds value to them as well. Amazon puts them in contact with customers. In fact, it is the reason that so many authors and publishers are in business today. Without Amazon, they would not be selling books.

Bill: Money, I certainly understand this. I sell books on Amazon. Amazon makes it very easy to do that. I am willing to pay Amazon to help sell my books.

Money: Yes, and this is a secret that most people just don't get. It is one of the big problems that independent business owners face. They just don't understand how to make money by "being the answer."

Bill: Money, can you explain that little bit more? This is a seriously huge point.

Money: No problem.

Let's take another example. Let's say that an individual wants to make money outside his/her job. We will refer to these people as Joe and Mary Jo—an ordinary couple. Joe and Mary Jo become members of a product distribution company. How can Joe and Mary Jo create value for the customer? Easily. The supplier is the company itself. It has the products and services that the customers need.

But, the company also has needs. The company must find a way to market and promote these products and services to the customers. This can be quite costly. They have to spend thousands (perhaps millions) of dollars on advertising. They also need a sales force. They need ways to communicate the benefits of the products and services to the customers. They need ways to let the customers know that the products or services that the company sells will solve a problem for the customers.

When Joe and Mary Jo became independent business owners with the distribution company, they became the ones who did the promotion and sales. This was extremely valuable to the company. For example, Joe and Mary Jo found the customers for the company and then showed the customers how to solve their problems by buying the products and services of the company. In addition to adding value and selling that value to the customers, Joe and Mary Jo sold their value to the supplier!

How does this work? Well, all companies expect to have costs in marketing and sales. But, they have a choice. What if they simply create a system that allows ordinary men and women to do the marketing and selling? There are a lot of advantages to this. Instead of being a nameless and faceless entity to the customers, the company now has a sales force that the customers know, like, and trust. And, the company only has to pay this sales force money if the sales force actually sells the products or services to the customers.

And, in the product distribution business, independent business owners also get paid when the people they recruit into the business make sales.

Bill: How does that work?

Money: Well, talk about adding value! Imagine how difficult it is for companies to find large numbers of independent salespeople for their products and services. Remember, in this model, the majority of the independent salespeople are selling small amounts. Instead of having a small sales force where each salesperson sells a lot of products/services, these companies have huge sales forces where each salesperson sells a smaller amount. Imagine how difficult it would be to recruit these people and train them and lead them? It would be a nightmare. That's why these companies reward their sales force members for recruiting other like-minded individuals.

Bill: Does this concept work for any kind of business? What about traditional businesses?

Money: Bill, this is simply how money is made. It does not work any other way. It works for every business in the world. It is how they make money.

The only thing that you get paid for is the value you add. You can add value down the value chain (to customers) or up the value chain (to suppliers).

Either way, you must make sure that the customers or suppliers perceive the value that you are giving them as true value. In other words, it doesn't matter what you think is valuable. It only matters what your customers and suppliers think is valuable.

When you sell something, you are simply adding up the costs of what you paid for that something and the value that you have added. This is what you sell. This is the selling price. These are the two things that are in the selling price. The portion you get to keep is the value you add.

That is how you make money. If you want to make *more money* then you either have to sell more or raise the value to the customer. That's it.

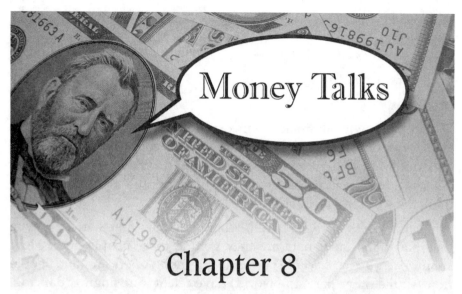

Chapter 8
Survivor, Money Edition

After Money and Bill Quain got to know each other better, and after Bill asked Money all the questions he wanted to ask, the two started talking about ways to help people understand their own situation better. As Money noted in the introduction, "Bill is a real master at making complicated ideas easy to follow." As it turned out, Money isn't so bad at it either!

Both Bill and Money like to talk about "learning to win the money game." To them, making money is a great game. But, unlike most other games, *everyone* can win at the money game. And like all other games, the money game requires some skill, and has some definite rules.

Bill and Money decided to use the "game" theme to help people understand what they need to undertake in order to become winners. Can you guess which reality show is most like the money game? Let's see if you chose the right one!

1. The *Real Housewives of New Jersey* (Beverly Hills, Timbuktu– or wherever)

2. *Dancing with the Stars*

3. *America's Got Talent*

4. *Naked and Afraid*

5. *Survivor*

Let's help you eliminate the incorrect answers. If you said *The Real Housewives of...* then you are wrong on two counts. First of all, Bill and Money don't think that has anything to do with the money game. (Unless you plan to marry for money.) Second, Bill and Money don't think the word *real* is quite accurate!

Dancing with the Stars? Well, when the show first started, maybe they had stars, but where are they getting these people now? How about *America's Got Talent?* There is no question: Americans (and people from all the other parts the world) have talent. But singing, dancing, juggling, and telling jokes aren't the talents we're talking about in this book. We are talking about a talent for making money.

Naked and Afraid? Neither Bill nor Money had ever seen the show, but as Bill put it, "I am afraid to watch it and I'm not even naked!"

No, the reality show that Bill and Money thought was the closest to the money game is *Survivor*. You know the show don't you? A group of people are put on an island someplace. They have to fend for themselves—hunting, fishing, building shelters, and starting fires. When all the conveniences of life are stripped away, it becomes quite apparent that some people are prepared to do everything it takes to survive, while some people just don't have the background and experience. When it comes down to surviving, the people on the island learn to depend on each other, but ultimately to look out for themselves. Of course on the actual show, there is only one winner in the end. That is one place where *Survivor* and the money game are different.

Bill put it this way:

"Most people couldn't survive too long on the island because they spent a lifetime depending on having things prepared for them: food already prepared and packaged. Homes built for them. There's nothing wrong with this—as long as the basic structure of society stays in place. It isn't until they get to that island that they have to prove they know how to survive."

Money says:

"The same principles apply in the money game. The world has become so corporatized that most people have no idea how to make money. They only know how to get a job and hold on to it. This is fine as long as there are no recessions or disruptions to their job market. The game is complicated by the fact that most people are in debt. Again, that's no problem as long as they keep their job and the paycheck keeps rolling in. But what happens if that job goes away? If they end up in survivor mode, and all they know how to do is ask for another job, they are competing with all those other people who got laid off. If they lack the skills to make money, they may never get off the island!"

Bill and Money together say:

Many people say that they are not worried about recessions because they have a real skill. They have something that is always going to be in demand. Okay, that's fair enough. We don't love that idea, but we can see how people depend on it.

But what about retirement? You see, while you can say that you might not be in survivor mode when you have a job, we contend that the crisis has already happened in terms of your retirement. What happens when the paychecks stop? Many people end up taking some kind of lower paying, non-glamorous job. Retired people take these jobs for two reasons. First, they need the money. Second, they have time on their hands and they miss being around other people.

But what if you could win the retirement game now—years before you retire?

People who win *Survivor: The Money Edition* are those who learn the secrets about making money. They aren't dependent on a corporation, a government, or a healthy rate economy. They are confident individuals who know they have the skills to continue bringing in money for as long as they want. You'll never get "voted off the island!"

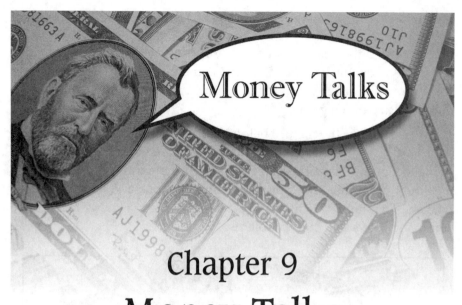

Chapter 9
Money Talks About Customers

Money had a lot to say about *customers*. In Money's opinion (and mine) customers are the only people who will give you money! Remember, Money can only go where he is commanded to go, and only people who *have* money can command him to go to you. For this reason, if you want more money, you have to get it from customers.

Do you remember the mistake that most people make in their financial lives? Their boss becomes their *only* customer. If you have *customers* however, you are never limited to just one. You can go out and find MORE of them. And, if you are smart, you will learn who the best customers are for your particular problem-solving set of products and services, and look for even MORE of these excellent creatures.

Everyone is Someone's Customer

Here is some great news. You already have a lot of experience with customers, because YOU are a customer. In fact, our entire economy is based on people working, making money, and spending that money on the things they need and want. You don't need to "get into this game" because you are *already* in this game. But now, you are trying to learn more about the behavior of customers so you can take part in a different part of the game.

Take a look at the picture below. You see that nice young couple in their car? They are going off to work. They are going to work all day to make money. They make a lot of money. That money gets "credited" into their accounts, and they take some of it out and stuff it in their pockets. That money is just sitting in their pockets, waiting for them to command it to solve their problems.

Now, look at the next picture and see people clapping and cheering for this young couple going to work. The clapping people own local restaurants, car dealerships, and grocery stores. You see, they know that nice couple comes into their shops as customers. They wouldn't be cheering if that nice young couple lost their jobs and stayed home and did not make money. No, that wouldn't fill their hearts with joy!

These merchants know that couple will soon have pockets full of money, and will be looking for ways to solve their problems. The restaurant owner has a "special" all set for tonight's menu. He knows exactly what that nice young couple likes to eat. The couple also has an anniversary this week, and the restaurant is hoping to sell them a bottle of champagne to celebrate their happiness. And, when that nice young couple commands some of the money to jump out of their pockets and jump into the restaurant owner's pockets, the restaurant owner will have a reason to celebrate as well.

The drycleaner is also excited. The restaurant owner is a customer of his, and needs fresh work uniforms. The restaurant owner commands money to the drycleaner. The uniforms are delivered in 24 hours, and the restaurant owner is happy.

Isn't the world a wonderful place? People go to work to make money. Once they have that money, they spend their time commanding it to go to other people. Would you like to be one of those receiving money? That can be arranged! You just need to find your *own* customers.

Learn the "Triggers" That Will Get People to Send You Their Money

Well, I have to tell you—human beings are never taught to do this. Yet, it is so fundamental to making money. "Triggers" are what get *potential* customers to turn into *actual* (buying and paying) customers. Learn the trigger words that will drive customers wild. You will be doing them a favor, because without those trigger words, they might not be inspired to solve their problem.

Let's say a company manufactures and distributes high-quality vitamins. Are there people who *want* this product? Of course. The people who want it are the people who want to be healthy, with more energy. Trigger words for these people might be how great will you feel, at the end of the day, when you still have energy for your family.

Here's another example. People use all sorts of tools (figuratively and literally) to solve their problems. If you want to dig a hole, you use a shovel. If you want to have a hole but did not have a shovel, you would buy a shovel to get that hole.

What might the trigger words be to attract that customer? How about "Get that garden into shape faster so that you can spend more time with your kids." Hey, wait a minute. Were you thinking the trigger words were going to be something about the *shovel*? Well, they could be, but those wouldn't be GREAT trigger words. They might work for some people. But, GREAT trigger words are always about the problem, not the tool.

In order to "trigger" a customer to send you their money, you must know what their problems are.

Money Talks about GREAT Customers

There are *good* customers, and there are *great* customers. You want to be in the kind of business that is suited for the *great* customers. After all, it doesn't take any more time to find a great customer instead of just a good customer, so why not?

Unfortunately, it is quite possible that you have never been trained or educated about identifying and attracting excellent customers.

Here are some of the things that make people GREAT customers:

1. They have money.
2. They have a problem that keeps coming back.
3. They have a desire to have someone else solve that problem for them again and again.

Can you see the importance of identifying customers who have a problem that keeps coming back? In this book, Money talks about building equity. One of the equities that Money recommends you build is customer equity. You build customer equity when you find a customer who has a problem that keeps coming back. If you solve that problem for the customer once, it is likely that they will ask you to do it again. This is equity.

When you find someone with a problem that keeps coming back, you can create *residual* income. In the two examples that Money used earlier in the chapter, one of the products was a one-time problem solution and the other one was a *residual* money-maker. Can you guess which one was residual?

Was it the shovel? No, the shovel is a one-time sale. (Nothing *wrong* with that. If you sell a shovel, it is better than selling nothing at all.)

Is it the vitamins? You guessed it. People who use vitamins that make them feel more energetic DO NOT want to start feeling tired again. They are going to *re-order* those vitamins so they can stay alert. This creates residual income.

Here is a problem that many people have. When they look for customers, all they can see are their friends and families. They think to themselves, "I don't want to try to make money from my friends and family members." This stops a lot of people dead in their tracks. Well, here are two ways to cure that problem.

1. Don't look for individual customers, look for business customers. Businesses need someone to help spread the word about their products. So, make the businesses your customers. Solve their problem again and again. No one minds taking money from a business, right? No one says, "I just feel so bad when that business

gives me money for helping them make more money." Problem solved. These are guilt-free customers!

2. Are your friends and family members spending money right now on things they need and want? Are they commanding money to jump out of their pockets and into the pockets of someone else because they need and want things to solve their problems? For example, do they buy groceries? Do they have a car? Do they have clothes? Do they have insurance? Of course they do! And if they are spending money on these things, it is because they have problems. You can be the one to solve their problems.

Not Everyone is the Right Customer for Your Solution

NEVER sell a solution to someone if it isn't right for them. But don't be the judge of that yourself! Let them decide. Present them with the solution to a problem they actually have. If they decide to solve their problem with you and your product—wonderful. But, don't decide for them. Let them be grownups.

A Final Word on Customers

In this chapter, Money talked about building a thriving business by helping customers solve their problems. Money did not say a single word about solving YOUR problems, right? Don't ever tell your customers about YOUR problems unless it is directly related to solving THEIR problems. For example, of you take vitamins, share that information—and more importantly, share the reasons you take those vitamins. This is all about them.

There is an old saying, "The best way to get what you want is by helping other people get what they want." In the end, it is all about helping others—and the people you want to help the most are the ones with money and a recurring problem.

THOSE people are great customers.

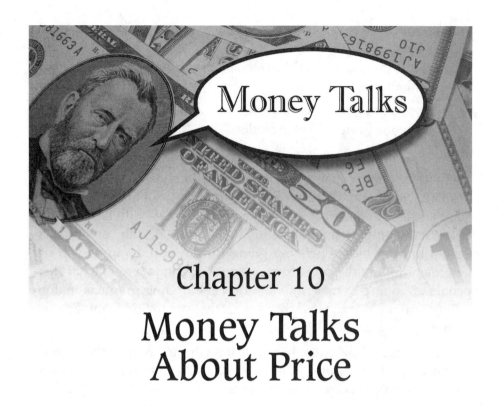

Chapter 10

Money Talks About Price

Okay, here is something that is actually going to grab you by the ears and shake you! Read this carefully and see what you are missing. I don't mean the word that you are missing. I mean the opportunity that you are missing. When you learn how some people are making money, and how you have been paying them—without knowing what the model is—it is going to be stunning.

Did you know that thousands of people around the world are making money by buying up inventory, changing the packaging, and selling products on Amazon? And, they are making a lot of money every single day. Remember, I am not suggesting that you go into this business, I simply want you to understand that price is not fixed and neither is added value.

Follow these steps and you will open the door to this idea:

1. Go to Amazon.com

2. On the search bar, under the category "Cells Phones & Accessories", search for "6 foot Universal USB Cell Phone

Cable Dark Green". (I love the color dark green. It goes so well with money!)

3. You should now see a page with about nine products on it, each one from a different seller.

Do you think that there are nine different manufacturers making a 6 foot dark green charger cable with a USB attachment on the end? I can almost guarantee you that there are not. I can almost guarantee you that some of those cables are exactly the same—with the exception of the packaging. (I can't absolutely tell you that with certainty, as I do not know which sellers are going to show up on any given day when you follow these instructions on Amazon.) Here is what these people are doing to make money: they are finding products that are selling well on Amazon and they search the web to find manufacturers of those products.

These sellers make sure they appear on the first page of the Amazon search by "adding value." Now, by default, your Amazon account might sort products by price. But even if that is so, all seven of those products on the first page have different prices. Why doesn't everyone just buy the lowest priced product?

Because, Amazon also rates by customer satisfaction. If I need a product quickly, and want one that works, I am more likely to buy from a seller who has a higher rating, even though that seller is charging a higher price. Of course, that's the whole reason that seller can charge a higher price—they built a good reputation among their customers. They built trust. This trust reduces risk. People will pay for risk reduction.

Your can charge a higher price when you add value!

People who are building businesses on Amazon (and other sites like eBay) don't have a single customer (like a boss)—they have thousands of customers. And, none of those thousands of customers cares how much money those sellers make. No, all those customers care about is that they get their cell phone charger as quickly as possible and that it works! Sure, they don't want to pay too much for it. But, they are willing to pay more if they can trust the seller, if other people say the product is reliable and worth the money, and if it gets there quickly. If they have a problem—and not being able to recharge your cell phone is a BIG problem—all they care about is getting it solved. The financial success of the company they buy it from is not important to them, EXCEPT that they want the company to stay in business so they can buy more stuff from them!

Did You Get That Last Point?
Your Customers WANT You To Make Money!!

Here is a fabulous point. Your customers not only want you to solve their problems, they want you to make money so that you will stay in business. Why is that? When your customers take the time to go online (or go to a store) to get information about a product and seller of that product, they are putting in effort. They are willing to invest their time because it means they will reduce their risk. Remember, when you reduce someone's risk, they give you money.

Your customer doesn't want to go to all the trouble of finding you, only to discover that you just went out of business. Now, they have to invest more time in order to find a seller that they can depend on. This increases their risk. This makes them unhappy. Do you want to make people unhappy? Of course you don't, so charge them enough money so that you will make a profit and be able to stay in business. What do we know about happy customers? They command money to jump out of their pockets and into yours.

What is The Problem with These Amazon Businesses?

While these Amazon businesses are a great example of how individuals can create a thriving business, there is a lot of risk associated with them. There are lots of competitors, no one will show you how to do it, you have to get listed on Amazon, and work hard to stay on the first page. You must be prepared to ship items, accept returns, and sell hundreds of different products.

All of these things add up to a big risk for you. I didn't tell you about this Amazon business so you would jump in. I wanted to show you how money can be made in today's economy. I simply want to reinforce the idea that you can add value and create thousands of customers simply by thinking differently. If you are working for someone else right now on a job (meaning you have one customer, your boss) you need to do something to *create a second stream of income that is not dependent on one customer*. You need to create hundreds, maybe even thousands of happy customers who want you to solve their problems, and who don't care how much money you make. In fact, you want to create thousands of customers who are loyal to you because of your reputation and trustworthiness.

What Should You Do?

Here is exactly what I want you to do. I want you to take the principles that the Amazon sellers use for their businesses, and use them to make money for yourself. But, I want you to reduce your risk, and immediately build system equity by finding a company that is looking for you. When you join that company, you can apply Money's seven secret steps to create a residual income that is based on the good wishes of thousands of customers.

Remember, it's not all about price.

Take a look at the Seven Secret Steps for making money. Do you see a step that says, "Always make sure to charge the lowest price so people like you"? It isn't all about price. It is all about value.

If you are having difficulty selling your products and services at a profitable price level, you need to raise the value. Concentrate on solving your customer's problems. You can do it.

Money Talks

Chapter 11

Money Talks About Using Good Examples to Add Value

By this time, we should have firmly established in your mind the importance of adding value in order to make money by selling that added value to your customers. Let's quickly review the adding value model.

VALUE ADDED

SUPPLIERS → **YOU** → CUSTOMERS

This is true for any business, so it's always great when you can discover something that adds value but does not add costs. The most valuable thing that you, as an independent business owner can add to your customer's perception of value is your good example. Generally, it has no cost associated with it so all of the added value the customer pays for is a direct profit for you.

Here is a Great Example of Adding Value Through Good Example

Suppose you become a member of a business that has everyday products that consumers need on a recurring basis. Your "good example" can have a massive impact on your bottom line. It costs you nothing, yet it produces incredible returns. Let's take several types of good example behavior and see how it adds value—and how it provides profits for you.

1. **You buy *and use* the products you represent.** How can you expect your customers to use your products and services to solve their problems if you do not? Your good example, although wordless, creates a resounding noise and clamor if it is negative, and a chorus of approval and applause if it is positive. Your behavior speaks volumes.

2. **You maintain an active role in your business, attend trainings, and you are a positive person.** These are all no-cost examples of good examples! Your affiliate partners will notice this. While they may not do what you do, they are almost certain not to do what you don't do. Again, this is fantastic added value.

3. **Use both your system and network equity in order to add value for the network affiliates in your line.** The beautiful thing about the equity that you get immediately after joining your business is the connection with more experienced leaders in your line. Again, this is tremendous added value that costs you nothing. It is supplied to you free of charge by the system at the network to which you belong.

Folks, very few people understand this, because they don't understand how money is made. They don't understand the basics of adding value. They think they are bothering people. They try to shelter their network affiliates. Instead, all they need to do is be a good example and say, "I believe in this!"

Bill Asks: Can you do it? Will you do it?

If you don't do it, you are giving up on several types of equity building. Money will tell you that if you don't do it, you are violating some of the most important principles of making money. You are deleting the value that you are selling to your customers, limiting the number of customers you have, and reducing the number of customers that your affiliates will bring to the business.

In the end, there is only one reason why you would not be a good example: YOU!

The good news: yesterday does not matter. Even today is a little sketchy. What matters is what happens in the next moment, the next day, the next month. Give yourself a break if you're feeling bad about something that you did or did not do in the business. It doesn't matter.

"But what about the customers and network affiliates I disappointed?" Here's a thought: do you think their problems have changed? Did the customers who wanted to use your products and services stop having problems? Did your network affiliates stop having problems? You may have disappointed them. You may have delayed their gratification. But they are still out there, waiting for you. Sure, maybe some of them will never come back, but some of them probably will. And even if you have to start over again, what does that matter? You started with zero before, right?

And how about the company that you are affiliated with? Would they still love you to help connect them with customers who need their products and services? Of course they would. Are they going to say, "Oh I'm sorry, you didn't do a great job the last time. We are firing you." No, they are not going to say that.

The greatest thing about becoming a good example—even if it is for the second or third time—is that you can do it by doing one easy thing—becoming a good example! You know what you have to do. So, let's do it.

Bill Quain Sums it Up

W ow, what a great experience this has been for me. I loved the time I spent with Money. Getting to ask him all those questions was fabulous. Learning his insights was really eye-opening. And spending all that time going through my notes in order to write this book—that was great too.

Now, it's time for me to sum it all up for you. But before I do, I want to tell you more about how I write books so that you will understand what this summary means to me—and what it can mean for you. You see, over the years I developed a certain method for writing my books. I make it a practice to never write the summary until I have finished the rest of the book, and then reread it. That way, I can pick up on all the bits of information that I feel are important for you.

I found a term hidden deep in the middle the manuscript that Money used to describe *exactly* what he had in mind when he advised us to combine a job and a personal business in order to create financial freedom. He referred to this as a *Financial Freedom Hybrid*. That is such a fantastic name for this system. A hybrid is a product or concept where the whole is greater than the sum of the parts. If you depend on a job it is unlikely that you'll ever have financial freedom. On the other hand, being an entrepreneur has many risks associated with it. But when you combine the two—building a new concept (a hybrid) out of the two parts, you end up with something that will help you grow, will protect you during uncertain times, and will allow you to realize fantastic rewards.

In some of my previous books, I wrote about the importance of having a job to support you while you built your business. I guess I had been talking about Financial Freedom Hybrids all along. But Money named it. Thanks to Money, I am proud to share the concept of the Financial Freedom Hybrid with you.

Now, let's spend a little time together as I summarize some of the really important points in this book. Remember, money is the most powerful tool we can use to both improve our personal lives and to affect change in our societies so that *everyone* can live better.

One Boss or Many Customers?

Right from the beginning of this book, Money began to lay out the vision and strategy for the Financial Freedom Hybrid. Money told us that it was much better to have many customers than one boss. When you only have one boss, anything that she/he decides is what you have to live with. If you have many customers, you don't need to worry if one of them isn't working for your best interest.

What is the difference between a boss and a customer according to Money? The most significant thing that I saw when I reread this book was Money's famous quote, "The difference between a boss and a customer is that a customer doesn't care how much money you make!" All your customers care about is whether or not you are able to solve their problems. They don't care how long it takes you—or doesn't take you—to come up with a solution. They are perfectly willing to pay you every time you solve their problems.

Your boss has less freedom than that. Your boss has other employees to worry about. If your boss pays you more than the other employees, the other employees are going to get upset. Everyone has to be paid on an average basis. And of course, your boss never wants to pay you more than she/he is getting paid. It's a real problem for people who want to make more money.

Finally, on most jobs, your boss is paying you for your time – not for the problems you solve. If you are supposed to work from 8 AM until 5 PM, your boss doesn't want to hear you say, "I finished my work at 3 PM so I am going home now." No, those are not the words a boss likes to hear. You see, your boss has paid you to work *for a certain amount of time*. If you finish your work early, the first thing that your boss is going to think is, "We need to give that person more work!" That's just the way it is.

Building the Five Equities

Money told us that we needed to build equity in order to create long-term wealth. You see, equity makes money for you, even when you have stopped working. The five equities that Money believes we should build are:

1. Self equity
2. Customer equity
3. Network equity
4. System equity
5. Mentor equity

Go back to Chapter 2 to look at that circular list of the five equities. It starts with self equity and ends up with mentor equity. All of these equities will create wealth for you, even when you are not working on them actively. If you want to build the personal business part of the Financial Freedom Hybrid, you must be able to recognize where equities exist, and then incorporate them into your personal business. Creating equities also works on the job, but remember, that is only one half of the Financial Freedom Hybrid.

Always start with self equity, and if you are helping anyone else build their business, get them started with self equity as well. How easy is it to build self equity? Well, let's put it this way: if you read this book, you created some beautiful self equity already! You develop self equity every time you are willing to look at things from a different perspective. If you do, you will be different than about 99.9% of the population.

In the end, you want to use the self, customer, network, and system equity you built as the foundation for your mentor equity. You can sell mentor equity. If you have mentor equity it will attract other great people to you. This is wonderful news. Some of this mentor equity has a piece in other people's businesses. You start getting a little bit of money every time the people that you mentor make money themselves. Even better, you can make money every time the people that *they* help to make money make money. This is how you build geometrically, using leverage.

Money did acknowledge that there was another kind of equity—investment equity. This is what most people think of when they think of building equity. These are stocks, bonds, mutual funds, etc. Money didn't want to discourage us from having investment equities. But Money pointed out that it was very unlikely that you are going to be able to create long-term financial security if your only plan was to invest your money in the stock market. All we have to do is look back over the past 20 to 30 years to see a number of times when that market crashed—taking a lot of investor dollars with it.

Almost Everyone is Living on a Fixed Income

I hope you saw Money's talk about fixed income! If I had a dollar for every time a retired person complained about "living on a fixed income" I would be a very, very wealthy man. But guess what? Anyone with a job is living on a fixed income. If you have a salary, you are going to be paid that salary. It is fixed. If you get paid by the hour, your salary is still relatively fixed. After all, how many hours a week can you work, and how many hours a week will they *let you work*? Even if you get overtime, you are still on a fixed income. How many hours per week of overtime will your boss give you? In the end, it is fixed.

Of course, that's if you are only building half of the Financial Freedom Hybrid. If you are only building the "job half" of the hybrid, you are definitely on a fixed income. That is why you need the other half of the hybrid! When you create a personal business, or build equities, you can un-fix your income in a positive way! If you have a financial need, you can always use your personal business to make more money. (Try doing that on a job!) Open your horizons. Make the process of making money possible. Get off that fixed income and get on with the business of making more money by building your hybrid.

Money Only Goes Where it is Commanded to Go

If you want more money, you must find someone who will command their money to go to you. That's it. End of story. This is one of the most important things that Money shared with us. I see so many people, waiting around for money, and then wondering why they never get any.

The people who send you money are called customers. Only a customer will send you money. Only a customer will command money to jump out of their pockets and into yours. Customers are wonderful people. You solve their problems, and they give you money. That's the way it works.

Some people say, "Well it is just such a pain in the neck to have customers. They always want things from me. It is so hard to get them to buy things. I'm always chasing after them, trying to get them to act."

All those things are true. Customers can be a pain in the neck. But remember, customers are never acting in *your* interest, they are acting in *their* interests. Customers are never going to give you money unless you give them value. They will trade their money for value.

If you have a boss, then you have a customer. The problem is, you only have one customer. If that one customer goes away—goes bankrupt, retires, quits, whatever—that's the end of your money-getting days! That's the danger of a job.

The Concept of Risk and Reward

There are three important concepts you need to pull from this particular chapter. Here they are:

1. One of the important reasons that you are going to build your Financial Freedom Hybrid is that it reduces your risks and maximizes your rewards. It reduces your risks because you still have the money that you make on your job coming in, but it maximizes your rewards because you are going to use equity to create a money-generating personal business. If you do it correctly, that personal business will also have low risks, because it will involve only a small monetary investment, and will come with built-in equity such as system and network equity.

2. People think that they are reducing their risk by having a job instead of being an entrepreneur. While this may be true in some cases, having all of your income coming from one source is a huge risk. If your company should go out of business, or if your boss decides that her favorite nephew should have your job, you could be out of luck!

3. When you begin to change your life by developing a personal business (building equity) you may be putting the people around you at risk. You are willing to assume some risk because you're getting rewards. However, the people around you may see your new attitude and ability to generate wealth as quite risky to their peace of mind. After all, if you are able to break out of the mold and gain financial freedom, this is going to put tremendous pressure on them. It will upset their whole notion of how to make money. Just be aware of this. It will help you to get through it when it happens.

Money's Seven Secret Steps for Making Money

While Money calls these the "Seven Secret Steps", there is one thing you need to keep in mind. There is no reason why these should be secret! Apparently, however, they are! They must be secret, because so few people seem to know what they are and how to use them. Here are the Seven Secret Steps:

1. Find a big problem

2. Determine if the people who have that problem also have money (these are your customers)

3. Identify a solution for the problem that your customers face (Don't reinvent the wheel)

4. Add value to the solution

5. Intercept the people with the pain and STIR that pain

6. Trade your solution to the pain for money

7. Relentlessly repeat steps 1 through 6

I particularly like step #7—Relentlessly repeat steps 1 through 6. I am always amazed at how most people will get up out of bed every morning and go to work, for 40 to 50 years of their lives, and never give it a second thought. Yet, when they hold the keys to financial freedom in their hand, they get excited about their new-found opportunity for short time, and then they drop off the face of the earth! Folks, you have to stick with it. You have to be relentless. This is an extra job. Is your future. Find a great company with great products, identify people with a problem, intercept them and STIR the pain, sell them the products as a solution to their problems, and then do it again, and again, and again. Remember, you are building a business.

Add Value to the Solution

Money was at his best in this chapter! What a concept! In order to make money, you need to add value. That value is only in the minds of the customers. It doesn't matter what you think is valuable.

Go back to Chapter 7 and look at that value formula. It starts with the supplier, goes to you where you add value, and then moves on to the customers. You can make money by adding value for customers at either end of the value chain. For example, you can add value for the end-users and they will pay you for it. The end-users are the customers on the far right side of the value chain. But you have another customer. It is the company that is selling the products. It is the distribution company. They will pay you when you create value for them.

Almost no one understands this. The reason that company is giving you money is because you are solving a huge problem for them. You are finding them customers. You are helping to develop a relationship between the customer and the products the company is selling. Those relationships end up with huge benefits for the company. This is a fantastic added value for the company.

When you bring new independent business owners to the distribution company, you get paid whenever one of your new owners does the same thing you just did. And in a wonderful example of leverage, you will get paid whenever one of the people you brought in brings in someone else—but only if those new people build customer relationships with end-users, and drive sales.

To Win the Money Game, You Need to Learn to be a Survivor

I really had to laugh when Money said that the money game was like the TV show *Survivor*. I didn't know Money watched TV. On *Survivor*, ordinary men and women are put in a very stressful situation where they need to learn to live off the resources of the land in order to have enough to eat, drink, and make a shelter. They and the other members of their tribe will face some arduous contests. Only the most resourceful will survive.

Well, the money game is just like that. Most people only know how to survive by finding a job and holding onto it. They haven't learned how to create wealth. They haven't learned to use their own wits—and the resources around them—to make money. If they lose their job, they lose their ability to make money.

However, after reading this book, you are now a survivor. You now know how to build a Financial Freedom Hybrid. You are a valuable member of your tribe! Congratulations survivor. You are a winner.

Find the Great Customers

If you are going to build a business by gathering customers, gather some great ones. The best customers need two things in order to be great customers. They need to have a problem—and they need to have money. Remember, you are going to make money by getting your customers to *command their money to jump out of their pockets and into yours*. It doesn't make much sense to ask someone with no money to try to put money into your pockets!

Great customers have great problems. The best problems for customers to have are problems that repeat themselves again and again. This helps to develop customer equity, and delivers residual income to you. Customers are all around you. Give them what they want and they will give you what you want. In fact, they will be happy to give up their money to get what they want.

Determine Your Price

You want to charge the highest price you can for the work you do. In order to do this, you have to determine how to add value specifically for the needs of your best customers. The more value you add, the higher price you can charge. You want to charge a higher price because it leaves more profit for you.

Always look for ways to raise the price or to sell more. Remember, if your customers pay more—and if they do it more than once—it means that they feel they are getting more. They want to get more. They love to get more.

Marketers use the following definition for price: "Price is everything you give up to get what you want." Convenience is a price. If your customers are inconvenienced when they try to buy something, it actually adds to the price as far as they are concerned. If you make it more convenient for them to buy the products or services you are selling, you are actually doing them a favor. *You are actually lowering the price.* (They give up less to get what they want!)

Use Your Own Good Example to Add Value

There are a couple of places in this book where you should get excited about how easy it is to build equity and make more money. The idea of creating self equity is one of those places. The idea of using your good example to create value in the minds of your customers is another one. Think about it. How easy is it to be a great example? You only have to do the things that you want your customers to do. If you want your customers to order a product on automatic delivery every month, you need to do it as well. If you want some of the people you bring to the business to work harder to build their businesses, then you must do it yourself first. If you want people to get trained, or to read books, or to be cheerful and optimistic, then you must be the example that drives their behavior.

Being a good example costs you nothing, but it has tremendous value to your business. Money believes in good example. Money has told me that money follows good example. It is a building tool. It is a leverage tool.

Never miss the opportunity to be a good example. Always do it. Always. That is how you make money.

Outtakes from My Conversation with Money – (Money Puts in his Own Two Cents)

As I spoke to Money hour after hour, I got to ask him some really interesting questions on your behalf. Money has some pretty strong opinions! Remember, he doesn't get involved in questions of fairness. Money doesn't have emotions. Money is able to look at each situation without prejudice.

Some of the topics that Money talked about in the "two cents" section are quite controversial. However, he applied his unique brand of logic to each situation. As Money explains it, "Human beings make everything complicated by letting emotions rule their money decisions. If you just look at these things logically, you can discover how to create real, long-lasting solutions for some of your biggest problems."

When you read his opinions in the "two cents" section, try to remain calm. Look at these things from Money's perspective. It's just the logical thing to do!

Have fun. Make money. Relax. And as Money would tell you, "Relentlessly do that again and again."

Outtakes from My Conversation with Money (Money Puts in his Own Two Cents)

#1 – Money Talks about the Income Gap

In recent years there has been a lot of talk about the "Income Gap." People are saying, "The rich are getting richer and the poor are getting poorer." In the United States, a recent poll showed that 69% of the citizens favored *taxes on the rich* as a way of redistributing wealth and reducing the gap.

Well, Money has two things to say about the "Income Gap". Here they are:

1. Yes, there is an Income Gap. But, it is not what humans think it is. It isn't the gap between what the rich are making and the poor are making. No! It is the gap between *what most people are making and what they COULD be making!* That is where the real Income Gap is!

2. Yes, there is an Income Gap between rich and poor, and it is getting wider. But, all that Money is going to say about that is this: If you think raising taxes on the rich is going to solve that problem, just read my thoughts on the Minimum Wage. That same logic applies to the idea that raising taxes on the wealthy will solve the Income Gap problem.

Okay, now let's get back to YOUR Income Gap problem. Let me repeat what I said above. YOUR Income Gap is the difference between what you are actually making and what you SHOULD be making. That is the ONLY Income Gap you should be worrying about right now. You see, if humans worried about their OWN Income Gap problem, and fixed it by simply making more money, then the OTHER Income Gap problem would be greatly reduced.

YOUR Income Gap

Every human being has the potential to attract and keep a lot of money. Most don't for the simple reason that they have bought into the myth that getting an education, finding a job, working hard, saving money, and investing in a retirement plan are the actual steps to having more money. If those WERE the steps, don't you think that more people would have more money? Of course they would. But, working hard at a job is NO GUARANTEE that you are going to reduce the Income Gap. In fact, it seems to be the very thing that is CAUSING the Income Gap.

Think about this. Poor people aren't making LESS today, are they? That isn't the problem, is it? No, the problem is that a few people are making MORE today—much more. This is why the gap is widening.

And YOUR Income Gap (the gap between what you are actually making and what you COULD be making) isn't widening because you are making less today, is it? NO!!!!!!

YOUR Income Gap is widening because the money you COULD be making has risen exponentially in the last few years. There are now so many NEW ways for ordinary human beings to make more money today that YOUR Income Gap is soaring out of control.

Ladies and gentlemen, human beings, if you are not participating in the absolute explosion of income-producing possibilities in the world today, you are missing out on one of the very biggest wealth-transfers of all times.

Look, did you ever look back on some trend, or gain in the stock market and say, "I wish I could have been there when it was first getting started. I could have made a fortune and been retired by now."? Yes, you did say that. I KNOW you did.

Well, guess what? TODAY IS THE DAY! It is not too late. This thing is just getting started. You are there at the right time, and at the right place. This is it.

Shrink YOUR Income Gap. Do it by getting into the game. Build your Financial Freedom Hybrid.

And what about "taxing the rich?" I'll bet you feel differently about that when you are actually saying, "Taxing the rich people *like me*."

#2 – Money Talks about the Minimum Wage

Humans are certainly getting riled up about the minimum wage issue. Politicians are trying to distract people from the real issues by pretending that the minimum wage argument will solve the money problem for millions of people. Those in favor of the minimum wage argue, "It isn't right that people work 40 hours a week and are still not able to support their families." This is a difficult issue, and a big distraction.

Let's Look at it Realistically

Let's say that the minimum wage is somewhere around $7.50 per hour. At 40 hours a week, that means that the minimum wage employee has a gross pay of $300 per week. This is about $15,000 a year. Is it fair that someone works hard for 40 hours a week, and 50 weeks a year, and only makes $15,000? With taxes, this is certainly not enough money to reasonably support even one person. If that person is a single parent with a family, there is no way they can live on $15,000 per year.

To cure this problem, some people (and the politicians who are getting all excited) say "Let's raise the minimum wage to $10 per hour." This raises the annual salary to about $20,000. Does that cure the problem?

There are several problems with this solution:

- If the employer is paying an extra hundred dollars per week, the employer is going to raise prices to cover those costs. Who pays those prices? The consumers (this includes minimum wage employees) do. Prices go up and it's soon time to increase the minimum wage again.

- But the big problem with this solution is that poor people (like the ones making minimum wage) have to pay a larger percentage of their income for the increased price. Rich people may not be affected so negatively when they have to spend another $10–$15 on weekly groceries. But to a minimum wage employee, that extra $10–$15 represents a significant portion of their pay.

Here is the Real Problem

People make $7.50 an hour because that is the value of their work. They have not developed any valuable skills that will help to *differentiate* them from the competition. And, at the minimum wage level, there is lots of competition. These are not bad people, of course not! It's just that their work is not as valued.

What Can We Do about This?

This may sound kind of harsh. But, the most important thing that you can do about minimum wage employees is to make sure you are not one of them. That's a basic truth. Instead, learn a lesson from the minimum wage controversy. Don't focus on public policy. Focus on adding value so that you can sell that value at a higher price. Create a residual income from the work that you do in addition to your job. Become a more valuable animal.

Once you and your family are secure, *then* you can decide to give some money to those less fortunate than you, or better yet, get involved in some kind of program that teaches people how to make money.

Teaching people to add value is a long-term solution to their problems.

Don't let the politicians get you distracted. You are on a mission.

#3 – Money on the Basics of Debit and Credit

At the beginning of our interview, Money said, "I can't believe that humans do not know how money works—a series of balancing debits and credits. After all, that's how the whole system works!"

Money has a great point. Debits and credits are the basics of money management and moneymaking. It isn't just a matter of getting money in (income) and keeping track of it as it goes out (spending). No, if you want to make money, and hold on to it, you must understand how people can actually track it, and most importantly, how debits and credits work when money moves around.

Money Talks about Debit and Credit Cards

I am so amazed most humans don't know what a credit or debit is. I'm not saying that people do not know the difference between a debit card and a credit card. Most of them do. I am saying that they don't understand the principles behind these cards, even though they use the words every day of their lives.

If I asked you, "Is that a debit card?" you would be able to say YES or NO with accuracy. But, if I asked you, "When you bought that new outfit yesterday, was your account credited or debited? Was the store's account credited or debited?" most humans wouldn't know the answer.

Debits and Credits—the basics

- Debit means, "To subtract."
- Credit means "to add."
- Whenever you have a debit, there must be an equal credit.

When something is added to one person's account, it must be subtracted from someplace else. Debits and credits, credits and debits. They are always in balance. It is how money moves through the system.

A Simple Example

Let's say that your job pays you $1,000 a week. At the end of the first week you receive a paycheck for $1,000. (This is a simple example so we will not be worried about taxes and other things like that.) Which account got debited and which account got credited?

If your paycheck is automatically deposited into your checking account, your account was credited with $1,000. In other words, since credit means "to add", your account now has a credit balance of $1,000.

On the other hand, when the money was transferred out of your company's account to pay you, their account was debited in the amount of $1,000 and the money was subtracted from their balance. Their balance in their account is now $1,000 less than it was before.

How did that money get into your company's account to begin with? They sold something to a customer. The customer's account was debited and your company's account was credited with the money. Debits and credits must always have a balance of zero.

Okay, How does a Credit Card Work?

Humans, if you can understand what I'm about to tell you here, you could experience a huge breakthrough in your understanding of money. But to do this, we have to introduce one more term—liability. You see, when someone extends you credit (which is what happens when you use a credit card) you are now in debt. You have a liability. Future earnings must cover that liability. In other words, every time you use a credit card you have signed a legal contract that says, "I am now in debt." I must pay this back. I agreed to pay back more than I borrowed. There is no way out of this. I will have to work tomorrow (and maybe for many "tomorrows") in order to pay off this debt.

Here's how it works in the language of money—debits and credits. Let's say you buy something for $100 and you use a credit card to pay for it. The credit card company sends $100 to the store. The credit card company's account is debited (money subtracted) and the store's account is credited (money added). That's how the actual money changes hand in debits and credits.

What happened to your account? No money was actually taken out of your account. After all, you have credit! There is an agreement between you and the credit card company. If they give you a credit line of $1,000, it means they will advance up to $1,000 in your name to any store you tell them to. But, your credit card agreement is like a balance. If you keep your balance with them at "zero" and your agreement is for a credit line up to $1,000, it means that you still have $1,000 worth of credit. But, when they sent that hundred dollars to the store for you in that example above, your balance is now -$100. Of course, if you don't pay it off immediately, your negative balance will be larger than $100 because you will also owe the credit card company interest. The longer you owe the money, the more interest you will owe on that money.

If you paid the hundred dollars off right away, you are, in a sense, crediting your account balance and bringing it back to zero. At this point, you still have $1,000 in credit available to you. Pretty simple, right? Well… for something so simple, credit card debt is a major problem for many humans.

#4 - Money Talks about Financial Slavery

Financial *FREEDOM* is great. The opposite of Financial Freedom is *Financial Slavery*. It is bad—very bad.

How do you get into Financial Slavery? You have DEBT. It is as simple as that.

You see, when you have debt, you give up choice. Free people have choices. Enslaved people do not. If you have debt (a mortgage, car payments, student loans, credit card debt, etc.) you HAVE to work in order to make your payments. If your boss says, "I want you to come in on the weekend to help us catch up on all this paperwork" you *have to do it* if you have debt. If you are thinking to yourself, "I have been working on this stupid job for twenty years without a decent vacation. I would really like to take a month or two off", you can't do it if you have debt. You need that paycheck!

If the industry you work in is having trouble, and your company is thinking about laying off people, you are terrified *if you have debt*. Isn't it terrible to be enslaved to worry and stress?

On the other hand, if you have another source of income, you might have choices. If you can make your house payments, car payments and other installment payments *without* the paycheck from your job, you have choices.

Best of all, if you have used the extra money your personal equity is bringing in to *pay off your debts,* you have REAL CHOICE.

Financial Freedom gives you choices. Financial Slavery takes them away.

Ironically, every single human has the choice to *seek* Financial Freedom. *Any* human being can achieve it. You can choose whether you want to live in freedom or slavery.

Which one will YOU choose?

#5 – Money Talks about Your 401(k) [Your 401(k) is Not Working? Hooray!]

How much money do you want to make? Let's put it this way, Money thinks you will be successful if your 401(k) is no longer working properly. What does Money mean by "not working properly"? It means that you didn't fall for the half-truths about your retirement.

Facts:

- 401(k) is a big tax advantage. And, you are crazy if you don't have one of these accounts—or some other tax-deferred retirement accounts.

- Financial advisors tell you that a 401(k) is great because it allows you to put money in now, while your tax rates are high, and allows you to take money out later (after you stop working) when your tax rates are lower. BUT, the financial advisors assume that you will be in a lower income tax bracket because they can't imagine how anyone could be in a higher tax bracket after they retire from their job!

Your Goal: Turn Your 401(k) into Your "Fun" Money

- What if you learned the secrets of making more money so that you never really "retire"? If you build your equity and turn it into a money-making, never-ending stream of income that continues to come in even if you stop working, then you can have it all.

- Your goal: create a fantastic equity-driven stream of income so that the *main advantage* of your 401(k) becomes completely unnecessary. The equity you built up is such a great residual income stream that your income is just as good after retirement as it was before!

#6 – Money Talks about Income Inequality

In recent years there have been many reports that women in the U.S. are paid less than men for the same job. In a recent television report, the commentator said that "the average woman was paid just 77% of what the average man received. This disparity was evident even in careers like nursing."

Wow, that seems bad, doesn't it? I mean, is that *fair*?

Why should women be paid less for the same work? Shouldn't there be a law to change this?

A law? No. If women are getting paid less than men, it is because their perceived value for that work is less than it is for men. That's how the marketplace works. The term "Equal pay for equal work" is misleading, because apparently, the people who are paying women for their work don't feel that the work women are doing is equal to the work men are doing.

STOP! Put down those matches. Don't burn this book! Money is not saying that this is fair. Remember, Money *never* uses the word "fair." Money is just money!

But, let's look at this situation and see how women CAN correct the inequity. In fact, let's see how they can make all the money they want—whenever they want it.

First of all, the television commentator in the report above said that the *average* woman makes just 77% of what the average man makes. Well, that word "average" makes me nervous. It means that *some of the women* are making less than the average man, and *some of the women* are making MORE than the average man. (Isn't that how averages work?)

So, if there is legislation to correct this situation, where is the final value going to come to rest? It will be with the *average man's salary*, so any woman who is making more will have to make less. In fact, any man who is making more will need to make less. Is that a solution? Probably not.

Is there a glass ceiling? Are there prejudices against women (and other minorities) when it comes to placing *value* on their work? Of course there is. It has been there forever. It will always be there, no matter how many laws are passed, or how much sensitivity training goes on. Prejudice is prejudice. It is a human flaw.

So, What Can Women Do?

There are two things to do. First, do whatever it takes to change the perception of YOUR value. Did you notice that I said "YOUR value"? That is the only thing you can control. If you are getting paid less than someone else, it *might* be because you have not established your value. Try building equity.

Second, you could just say, "This is terrible, and I am not going to spend my time trying to work against a system that is working against me." I think this is the smarter thing to do. Who wants to waste time trying to change *someone else's mind*? Most of the time, it doesn't work.

It is time to put your Financial Freedom Hybrid plan into action. It is time to start thinking of your job as simply a place where you get the basics fulfilled – a salary, insurance, paid vacation days, etc. NOW, START BUILDING YOUR OWN BUSINESS ON THE SIDE. In the long run, you will be so much better off.

Is it hard to let go of the *legitimate* anger you are feeling about the situation? Of course it is. But always remember this—when you start fighting the prevailing powers of unfairness, you *give power in your life to those same people*! They start to consume your thinking. They are in your head all the time. This gives them power over you! They are already paying you too little. Do you want them to be in your head 24/7 as well?

And by the way, when you are financially free, put your feet up at work and take a little break. After all, YOU have the power now!

#7 – Money Says You'll Never Get Rich If You Have a Big But...

Okay humans, calm down. I didn't say "You'll never get rich if you have a big *butt*", I used the word "but"!

A lot of rich people have big butts, but NONE of them have big buts. What is a "but"? It is an excuse, as in the following:

I like to be rich, *but...*

- I don't have the time to do it right now
- I don't know how to do it
- I don't want to be mean like rich people are
- People like me are never rich
- My brother-in-law says this is a bad idea
- Etc.

You see, the BIG BUT that is keeping you from getting rich (or whatever goal you want to set for yourself) is just an excuse. Thousands of people become wealthy every year. They are ordinary men and women, just like you. What is the big difference between them and you? They stopped making excuses.

Look, sometimes there are valid excuses for putting off your dreams and ambitions. Stuff happens! But how *long* will you put things off? When will you start getting rid of all the excuses you have been making, and start stuffing your pockets with money?

A few years ago, Bill Quain wrote a book called *10 Rules to Break & 10 Rules to Make: The Do's and Don'ts for Designing Your Destiny*. One of Bill's *Rules to Break* is "Accept Valid Excuses." In this chapter, Bill listed 10 excuses, and his rebuttal for each one. Here is a sample of some of Bill's favorites.

Excuse: I come from an underprivileged background.

Rebuttal: That's too bad, do you want your children to come from one as well?

Excuse: There aren't enough hours in the day.

Rebuttal: How many hours did you get yesterday? *Everyone* gets 24 of them. It all depends on how you use them.

Excuse: People like me never succeed.

Rebuttal: You are right! Stop being someone like you and start being like successful people.

Excuse: I'm too young to be taken seriously.

Rebuttal: That's too bad, your energy and youthfulness would have been real assets for you. Grow up.

Excuse: I'm too old to try anything new.

Rebuttal: That's too bad. Your wisdom and experience would have benefited all of us. Rest in Peace.

You see folks, *everyone* has excuses. But do you know what NO ONE has? *No one has both excuses and money.* When it comes to money and excuses, you need to give up one of them. Do you really need help deciding which one to give up?

You can have a "but-load" of excuses or a "boat-load" of riches. Get rid of that Big But, and start making more money!